United States Government Accountability Office

Report to the Committee on Energy and Natural Resources, U.S. Senate

September 2013

COMPACTS OF FREE ASSOCIATION

Micronesia and the Marshall Islands Continue to Face Challenges Measuring Progress and Ensuring Accountability

GAO Highlights

Highlights of GAO-13-675, a report to the Committee on Energy and Natural Resources, U.S. Senate

COMPACTS OF FREE ASSOCIATION

Micronesia and the Marshall Islands Continue to Face Challenges Measuring Progress and Ensuring Accountability

Why GAO Did This Study

In 2003, the U.S. government approved amended Compacts of Free Association with the FSM and the RMI, providing for a total of $3.6 billion in assistance over 20 years. Given the countries' dependence on compact funding, GAO was asked to conduct a review of the use and accountability of these funds. This report addresses (1) the FSM's and RMI's use of compact funds in the education and health sectors; (2) the extent to which the FSM and RMI have made progress toward stated goals in education and health; and (3) the extent to which oversight activities by the FSM, RMI, and U.S. governments ensure accountability for compact funding. GAO also provided information on infrastructure spending and projects in the education and health sectors. GAO reviewed relevant documents and data, including single audit reports; interviewed officials from Interior, other U.S. agencies, and the FSM and RMI; assessed data reliability for subsets of both countries' education and health indicators; and visited compact-funded education and health facilities in both countries.

What GAO Recommends

Among other actions, Interior should (1) take all necessary steps to ensure the reliability of FSM and RMI indicators in education and health, (2) assess whether to designate each country as high risk, and (3) take actions to correct its disproportionate staffing shortage related to compact grant implementation and oversight. Interior generally agreed with GAO's recommendations and identified actions taken, ongoing, and planned.

View GAO-13-675. For more information, contact David Gootnick at (202) 512-3149 or gootnickd@gao.gov.

What GAO Found

In fiscal years 2007 through 2011, the Federated States of Micronesia (FSM) and the Republic of the Marshall Islands (RMI) spent at least half their compact sector funds in the education and health sectors. Because both countries spent significant amounts of compact funds on personnel in the education and health sectors, the U.S.–FSM and U.S.–RMI joint management and accountability committees capped budgets for personnel in these sectors at fiscal year 2011 levels due to concerns about the sustainability of sector budgets as compact funding continues to decline through fiscal year 2023. The FSM states completed plans to address annual decreases in compact funding; however, the FSM National Government and the RMI have not submitted plans to address these annual decreases as required. Without plans, the countries may not be able to sustain essential services in the education and health sectors in the future.

Data reliability issues hindered GAO's assessment of progress by the FSM and RMI in the education and health sectors for fiscal years 2007 through 2011 for the compacts as a whole. Between 2004 and 2006, both countries began tracking education and health indicators, establishing data collection systems, and collecting data for the majority of the indicators and have continued to track data on their indicators since that time. In education, GAO found 3 of 14 indicators in the subsets of indicators it reviewed for both countries to be sufficiently reliable and 1 also to be capable of demonstrating progress: the education level of teachers in the RMI. GAO found a variety of data reliability problems, such as some FSM states reporting data for both public and private schools while other states included only public schools in their data. In the health sector, GAO determined that data for all 5 of the subset of indicators it reviewed in the FSM were not sufficiently reliable to assess progress for the compacts as a whole, and in the RMI, 1 health indicator was sufficiently reliable and 2 were not sufficiently reliable; for 2 other RMI health indicators, GAO had no basis to judge. In much of their reporting on their education and health indicators, the FSM and RMI have noted data reliability problems and some actions they have taken to address the problems. The U.S.–FSM and U.S.–RMI joint management and accountability committees have also raised concerns about the reliability of FSM's education and health data and RMI's health data and required that each country obtain an independent assessment and verification of these data; both countries have yet to meet that requirement, and, as a result, neither country can determine its progress in these sectors.

The single audit reports GAO reviewed indicated challenges to ensuring accountability of compact and noncompact U.S. funds in the FSM and RMI. For example, the governments' single audits showed repeat findings and persistent problems in noncompliance with U.S. program requirements, such as accounting for equipment. The Department of the Interior (Interior) has taken steps regarding accountability of compact funds such as establishing the Chuuk Financial Control Commission, but Interior has not coordinated with other U.S. agencies about the risk status of the FSM and RMI. Furthermore, the FSM, RMI, and U.S. offices responsible for compact administration faced limitations hindering their ability to conduct compact oversight. For example, Interior's Office of Insular Affairs (OIA) experienced a staffing shortage that disproportionately affected compact grant oversight compared to other OIA activities, with 5 of 11 planned positions filled.

Contents

Tables

Figures

Abbreviations

CFCC	Chuuk Financial Control Commission
Education	U.S. Department of Education
EPPSO	Economic Policy, Planning, and Statistics Office (RMI)
FAC	Federal Audit Clearinghouse
FSM	Federated States of Micronesia
HAFSM	U.S. Army Humanitarian Assistance Program for the FSM
HHS	U.S. Department of Health and Human Services
Interior	U.S. Department of the Interior
Labor	U.S. Department of Labor
JEMCO	Joint Economic Management Committee (FSM)
JEMFAC	Joint Economic Management and Financial Accountability Committee (RMI)
MDG	Millennium Development Goals
OAG	Office of the Auditor-General (RMI)
OCI	Office of Compact Implementation (RMI)
OIA	Office of Insular Affairs
OMB	Office of Management and Budget
ONPA	Office of the National Public Auditor (FSM)
OPA	Office of the Public Auditor (Pohnpei State, FSM)
PMU	Program Management Unit (FSM)
portfolios	Ministry of Education annual portfolio budget statements (RMI)
RMI	Republic of the Marshall Islands
SBOC	Office of Statistics, Budget and Economic Management, Overseas Development Assistance, and Compact Management (FSM)
SPC	Secretariat of the Pacific Community
State	U.S. Department of State

GAO U.S. GOVERNMENT ACCOUNTABILITY OFFICE

441 G St. N.W.
Washington, DC 20548

September 20, 2013

The Honorable Ron Wyden
Chairman
The Honorable Lisa Murkowski
Ranking Member
Committee on Energy and Natural Resources
United States Senate

In 2003, the U.S. government approved amended Compacts of Free
Association with the Federated States of Micronesia (FSM) and the
Republic of the Marshall Islands (RMI).[1] These amended compacts
provide for a combined total of $3.6 billion in U.S. grant assistance for the
two countries over 20 years from fiscal year 2004 through fiscal year
2023. The first half of this 20-year grant period will be completed at the
end of September 2013. The amended compacts state that the purpose
of the grant funds is to assist the FSM and RMI governments in their
efforts to promote the economic self-sufficiency and budgetary self-
reliance of their people. Under the compacts, U.S. grant funding
decreases annually in most years while, at the same time, contributions to
trust funds for the FSM and the RMI increase; earnings from the trust
funds are intended to provide an annual source of revenue after the
grants end in 2023.[2]

In 2006, we reported that since enactment of the amended compacts in
2004, the FSM and the RMI had made efforts to meet the requirements
for implementation, performance measurement, and oversight. However,
both countries faced challenges in planning for sustainability, measuring
progress, and ensuring accountability.[3] You requested that we conduct a

---

[1] Compact of Free Association Amendments Act of 2003, Pub. L. No. 108-188 (Dec. 17,
2003).

[2] See GAO, *Compacts of Free Association: Trust Funds for Micronesia and the Marshall
Islands May Not Provide Sustainable Income*, GAO-07-513 (Washington, D.C.: June 15,
2007).

[3] See GAO, *Compacts of Free Association: Micronesia and the Marshall Islands Face
Challenges in Planning for Sustainability, Measuring Progress, and Ensuring
Accountability*, GAO-07-163 (Washington, D.C.: Dec. 15, 2006). We issued this report to
comply with a reporting mandate in the amended compacts' implementing legislation,
which Congress later eliminated. (Pub. L. No. 108-188, § 104(h), as amended by Pub. L.
No. 111-68, § 1501(c), Oct. 1, 2009).

GAO-13-675 Compacts of Free Association

review of the use and accountability of amended compact funds in the FSM and RMI since our prior report. In this report, we examine

1. the FSM's and RMI's use of compact funds in the education and health sectors;

2. the extent to which the FSM and RMI have made progress toward achieving their stated goals in education and health; and

3. the extent to which oversight activities by the FSM, RMI, and the United States ensure accountability for compact funding.

In addition, we provide information on the FSM and RMI infrastructure sector grants in appendix II.

To examine the countries' use of compact funds in the education and health sectors, we reviewed available expenditure data in the FSM and RMI single audits for fiscal years 2007 through 2011. To evaluate the extent to which the FSM and RMI have made progress toward achieving their stated goals in the education and health sectors, we reviewed subsets of FSM and RMI performance indicators that were cited in (1) the U.S. government's 5-year reviews of the FSM and the RMI amended compacts,[4] (2) U.S.–FSM Joint Economic Management Committee (JEMCO) and U.S.–RMI Joint Economic Management and Financial Accountability Committee (JEMFAC) health- and education-related resolutions, or (3) the United Nations Millennium Development Goals performance measures.[5] We then reviewed the data for the subsets of indicators in the FSM and RMI annual reports for 2007 through 2011. To examine oversight activities, we observed the 2012 annual meetings, the 2013 midyear meetings, and the 2013 annual meetings of the JEMCO and the JEMFAC, which allocate grants and provide oversight for the amended compacts. We also reviewed FSM and RMI single audits for

---

[4]According to the compacts' implementing legislation, the United States is required to submit annual reports on the 5th, 10th, and 15th anniversaries of the enactment of the law that review the terms of the respective compacts and consider the overall nature and development of the U.S.–FSM and U.S.–RMI relationships.

[5]The United Nations Millennium Development Goals and their respective performance measures aim to meet the needs of the world's poorest individuals. All of the world's countries and leading development institutions have agreed to observe and pursue these goals and performance measures.

fiscal years 2006 through 2011.[6] In addition, we interviewed officials from the Departments of the Interior (Interior), Health and Human Services (HHS), Education (Education), and State (State). We also interviewed FSM national and state officials and RMI officials in the health, education, and infrastructure sectors, and we directly observed selected compact-funded education and health facilities in Chuuk and Pohnpei states in the FSM and Majuro and Kwajalein Atolls in the RMI.[7] The observations we made during our site visits to facilities such as hospitals, dispensaries, and schools in the FSM and RMI are not generalizable. We determined that the financial data examined in this report are sufficiently reliable for our purposes. However, our reviews of performance data from both the FSM and RMI and interviews with FSM and RMI officials revealed important limitations in the data in the countries' annual reports on education and health indicators, and therefore we determined that many of these data were not sufficiently reliable for the purpose of measuring progress for the compacts as a whole over our time frame. For additional details on our objectives, scope, and methodology, see appendix I.

We conducted this performance audit from August 2012 to September 2013 in accordance with generally accepted government auditing standards. Those standards require that we plan and perform the audit to obtain sufficient, appropriate evidence to provide a reasonable basis for our findings and conclusions based on our audit objectives. We believe that the evidence obtained provides a reasonable basis for our findings and conclusions based on our audit objectives.

Background

The FSM and the RMI are located in the Pacific Ocean just north of the equator, about 3,000 miles southwest of Hawaii and about 2,500 miles southeast of Japan (see fig. 1). The FSM is a federation of four semiautonomous states and has a population of approximately 103,000 (as of 2010) scattered over many small islands and atolls. The FSM states maintain considerable power, relative to the FSM National

---

[6]The scope for this report is generally fiscal years 2007 through 2011; however, we are including fiscal year 2006 because the last single audit report discussed in our prior report (GAO-07-163) was for fiscal year 2005.

[7]In the FSM, we focused our review on the National Government and the state governments of Chuuk and Pohnpei. Chuuk and Pohnpei account for 82 percent of the total population of the FSM. We did not include in our review the state governments of Yap and Kosrae.

Government, to allocate U.S. assistance and implement budgetary policies. Chuuk, the largest state, has 47 percent of the FSM's population, followed by Pohnpei (35 percent), Yap (11 percent), and Kosrae (6 percent).[8] By contrast, the RMI government is responsible for allocating U.S. assistance in that country, though the RMI's 29 constituent atolls and five islands exercise local government authority. About three-quarters of the RMI population of approximately 53,000 (as of 2011) live in Majuro, the nation's capital, and on Ebeye Island in the Kwajalein Atoll.

---

[8]Percentages may not add up to 100 due to rounding.

Figure 1: Location and Map of the Federated States of Micronesia and the Republic of the Marshall Islands

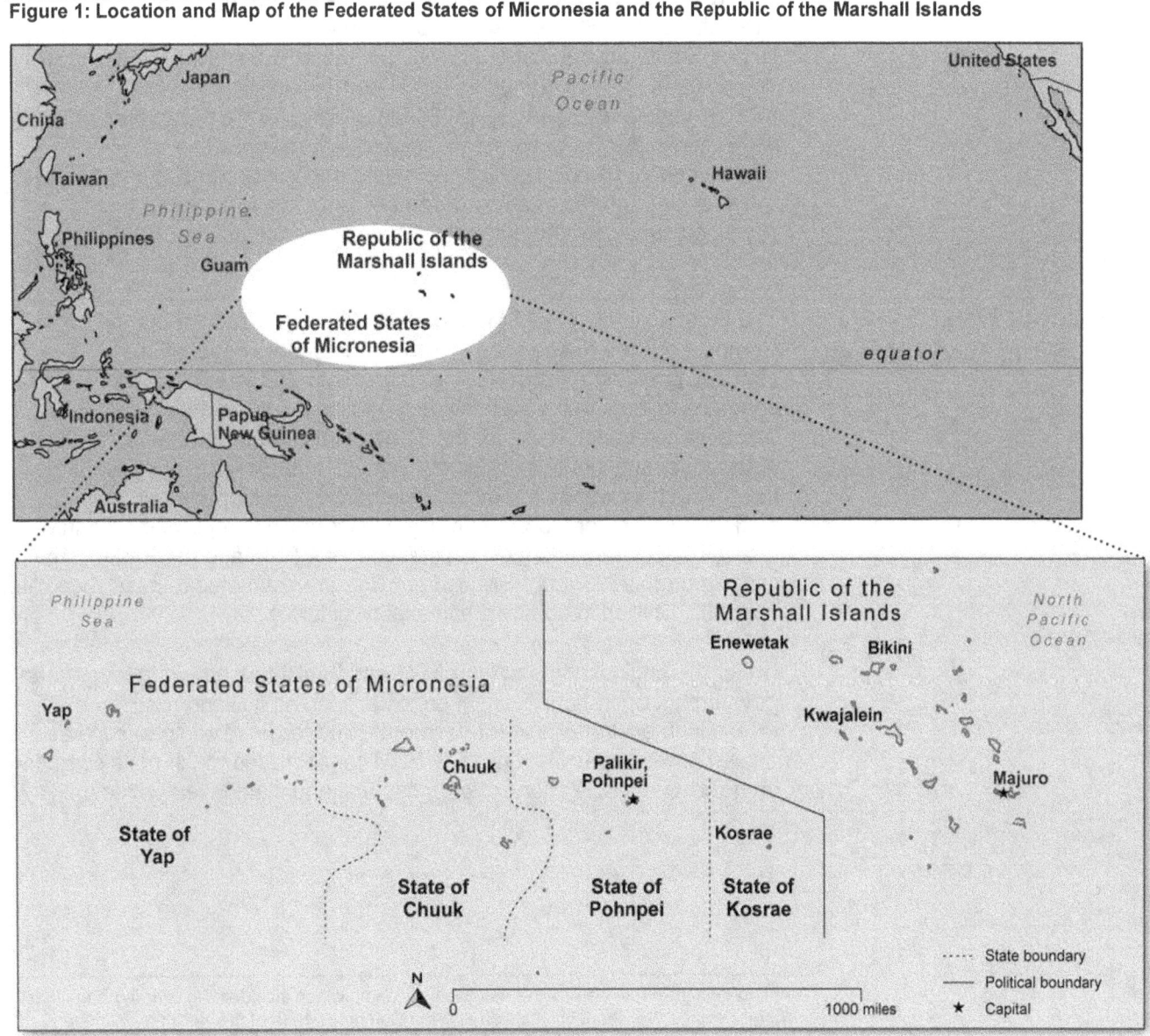

Sources: GAO presentation from Map Resources and National Oceanic and Atmospheric Administration (maps).

GAO-13-675 Compacts of Free Association

U.S. relations with the FSM and the RMI began during World War II, when the United States ended Japanese occupation of the region. The United States administered the region under a United Nations trusteeship beginning in 1947.[9] During the 1940s and 1950s the RMI was the site of 67 U.S. nuclear weapons tests. The four states of the FSM voted in a 1978 referendum to become an independent nation, while the RMI established its constitutional government and declared itself a republic in 1979. Under the trusteeship agreement, both newly formed nations remained subject to the authority of the United States until 1986.

Compact of Free Association: 1986 through 2003

The United States, the FSM, and the RMI entered into the original Compact of Free Association in 1986 after lengthy negotiations. The compact provided a framework for the United States and the two countries to work toward achieving the following three main goals: (1) establish self-government for the FSM and the RMI, (2) ensure certain national security rights for all of the parties, and (3) assist the FSM and the RMI in their efforts to advance economic development and self-sufficiency. The compact's third goal was to be accomplished primarily through U.S. direct financial assistance to the FSM and the RMI. From 1987 through 2003, the FSM and the RMI are estimated to have received about $2.1 billion in compact financial assistance.[10]

Under the original compact, the FSM and the RMI used funds for general government operations; capital projects, such as building roads and investing in businesses; debt payments; and targeted sectors, such as energy and communications. The FSM concentrated much of its spending on government operations at both national and state levels, while the RMI

---

[9]This was the Trust Territory of the Pacific Islands, which included the island groups that later became the Republic of Palau and the Commonwealth of the Northern Mariana Islands, as well as the FSM and RMI. The Department of the Navy began civil administration of all these islands on July 18, 1947. This responsibility was transferred to Interior in July 1951.

[10]This estimate represents total nominal outlays. It does not include payments for compact-authorized federal services or U.S. military use of Kwajalein Atoll land, nor does it include investment development funds provided under section 111 of Pub. L. No. 99-239, the law enacting the original Compact of Free Association in 1986.

emphasized capital spending.[11] While the original compact set out specific obligations for reporting and consultations regarding the use of compact funds, the FSM, RMI, and U.S. governments provided little accountability over compact expenditures and did not ensure that funds were spent effectively or efficiently.[12]

Amended Compacts of Free Association: 2004 through 2023

In 2003, the United States approved separate amended compacts with the FSM and the RMI that went into effect on June 25, 2004, and May 1, 2004, respectively.

Financial Assistance

The amended compacts provide for direct financial assistance to the FSM and the RMI from 2004 to 2023, decreasing in most years (hereafter referred to as the annual decrements). The amounts of the annual decrements are to be deposited in the trust funds established under the amended compacts for the two nations (see fig. 2).[13] For more information on compact assistance and trust fund contributions, see appendix III.

---

[11]See GAO, *Foreign Assistance: U.S. Funds to Two Micronesian Nations Had Little Impact on Economic Development*, GAO/NSIAD-00-216 (Washington, D.C.: Sept. 22, 2000). We reported that FSM and RMI compact funds spent on general government operations maintained high government wages and a high level of public sector employment, discouraging private sector growth, and that compact funds used to create and improve infrastructure likewise did not contribute to significant economic growth.

[12]In addition, under the original compact, the FSM and RMI also benefited from numerous U.S. federal programs and citizens of both nations exercised their right under the compact to live and work in the United States as "nonimmigrants" and to stay for long periods. Nonimmigrant status typically signifies nonpermanent visitors, such as tourists or students. See GAO, *Foreign Assistance: Effectiveness and Accountability Problems Common in U.S. Programs to Assist Two Micronesian Nations*, GAO-02-70 (Washington, D.C.: Jan. 22, 2002); and *Compacts of Free Association: Improvements Needed to Assess and Address Growing Migration*, GAO-12-64 (Washington, D.C.: Nov. 14, 2011).

[13]The amended compacts require the FSM and the RMI to make onetime contributions of $30 million each to the trust funds; these initial investments occurred in August 2006 and September 2005, respectively. The amended compacts' implementing legislation provides a continuing appropriation until 2023 for the financial assistance.

Figure 2: U.S. Grant Assistance and Trust Fund Contributions to Be Provided to the Federated States of Micronesia (FSM) and the Republic of the Marshall Islands (RMI) under the Amended Compacts, Fiscal Years 2004 through 2023

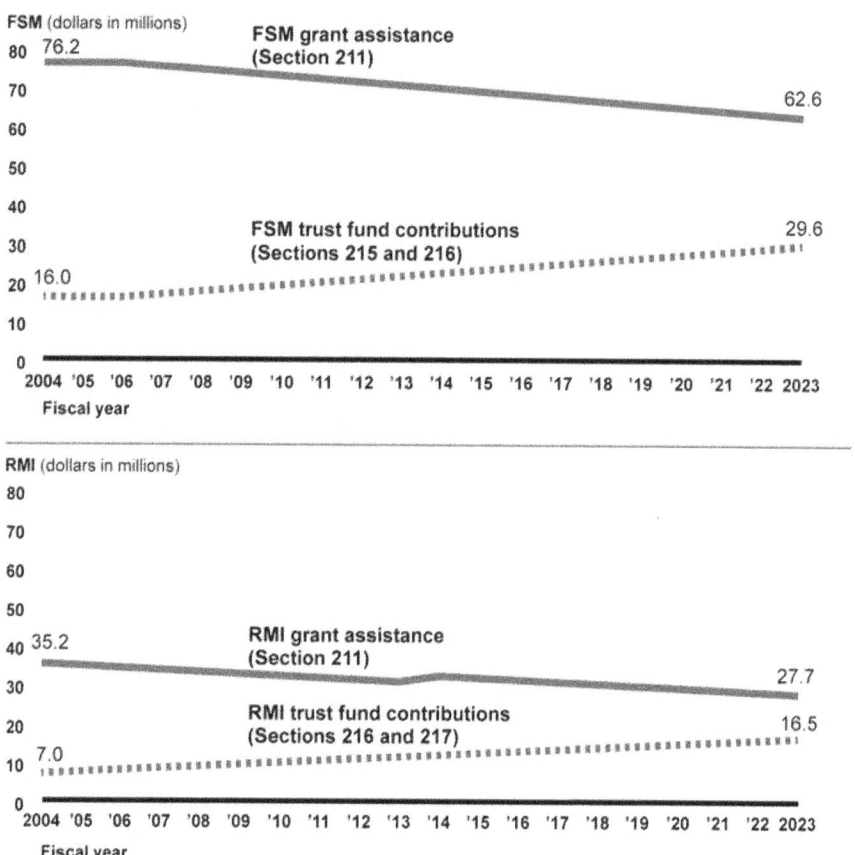

Source: Compacts of Free Association as Amended, Between the Government of the United States of America and the Government of the Federated States of Micronesia and the Government of the Republic of the Marshall Islands, Pub. L. No. 108-188.

Notes: Sections 211 of the amended compacts detail grant assistance to the FSM and the RMI, while Sections 215 and 216 of the U.S.–FSM compact and sections 216 and 217 of the U.S.–RMI compact detail contributions to the FSM and RMI trust funds. See Pub. L. No. 108-188. These dollar amounts shall be adjusted each fiscal year for inflation by the percentage that equals two-thirds of the percentage change in the U.S. gross domestic product implicit price deflator, or 5 percent, whichever is less in any one year, using the beginning of 2004 as a base. Grant funding can be fully adjusted for inflation after 2014, under certain U.S. inflation conditions. The increase in RMI grant assistance from fiscal year 2013 to 2014 is due to a $2 million increase in payments to be made available for addressing the special needs of the community at Ebeye and other Marshallese communities within the Kwajalein Atoll.

GAO-13-675 Compacts of Free Association

The amended compacts and associated fiscal procedures agreements[14] require that grant funding support the countries in six core sectors—education, health, infrastructure, environment, private sector development, and public sector capacity building[15]—with the education and health sectors having the greatest priority. Within the core sector grants, the RMI must also target grant funding to Ebeye and other Marshallese communities within Kwajalein Atoll: $3.1 million annually for 2004 through 2013 and $5.1 million annually for 2014 through 2023 (hereafter referred to as Ebeye special needs funds).[16]

In addition to receiving compact sector grants, the FSM and the RMI are eligible for a supplemental education grant each year.[17] The amended compacts' implementing legislation authorized annual appropriations of about $12.2 million for the FSM and $6.1 million for the RMI beginning in 2005 to the U.S. Secretary of Education to supplement the education grants awarded under the amended compacts. Under the fiscal procedures agreements, permitted uses of the supplemental education grant funds include, among other things, support for direct educational services at the local school level focused on school readiness, early childhood education, primary and secondary education, vocational training, adult and family literacy, and the smooth transition of students from high school to postsecondary educational pursuits or rewarding career endeavors. Funding for the supplemental education grant is appropriated annually to Education and transferred to Interior for

---

[14]The agreements between the U.S. government and the FSM and RMI governments contain detailed requirements concerning implementation of the amended compacts' funding and accountability provisions.

[15]Other sectors can be established. In 2012, the United States and the FSM created the enhanced reporting and accountability sector and in fiscal years 2012 and 2013 supported it with grant funds aimed at developing and implementing systems, financial management procedures, and internal controls that account for and ensure reporting on the use of amended compact funds. This grant can only be continued by mutual agreement between the United States and the FSM; otherwise, the grant ends after fiscal year 2014.

[16]Section 211(b)(1) of the U.S.–RMI amended compact details how grant funding should be allocated for Ebeye special needs. Additional assistance for the Kwajalein Atoll is outlined in sections 211(b)(2) and 212, which provide $1.9 million to address special needs, with an emphasis on Kwajalein landowners, and $15 million annually starting in 2004, rising to $18 million in 2014, for U.S. military use and operating rights. The RMI government uses the funds to compensate landowners on the Kwajalein Atoll.

[17]The supplemental education grant is awarded in place of grant assistance formerly awarded to the countries under several U.S. education, health, and labor programs.

disbursement, with Interior responsible for ensuring that the use, administration, and monitoring of supplemental education grant funds are in accordance with a memorandum of agreement among Interior, Education, HHS, and the Department of Labor (Labor), as well as with the fiscal procedures agreements.[18]

In addition to amended compact grants, the FSM and the RMI receive other grants and assistance from U.S. agencies. For example, in fiscal years 2007 through 2011, the FSM spent about $197 million and the RMI spent about $46 million in noncompact grants from agencies including Interior, Education, HHS, Labor, and the Department of Transportation. See appendix IV for more information on noncompact grants awarded to the FSM and the RMI.

Amended Compacts Oversight and Administration

The legislation and fiscal procedures agreements for the amended compacts established oversight mechanisms and responsibilities for the FSM, RMI, and the United States.

Joint Management and Accountability Committees

JEMCO and JEMFAC were jointly established by the United States and, respectively, the FSM and the RMI to strengthen the management and accountability and promote the effective use of compact funding. Each five-member committee comprises three representatives from the United States government and two representatives from the corresponding country.[19] The United States, the FSM, and the RMI are required to provide the necessary staff support to their representatives on the committee to enable the parties to monitor closely the use of assistance

---

[18]The provision authorizing the supplemental education grant in the amended compacts' implementing legislation authorizes to be appropriated to the Secretary of Education an annual amount adjusted for inflation (partial) through 2023. A memorandum of agreement among Interior, Education, HHS, and Labor states that Education "shall seek the annual appropriation of funds for the supplemental education grants, including adjustments for inflation, as described in Section 105(f)(1)(B)(iii) of Pub. L. No. 108-188." According to Education officials, the department has not sought the inflation increases due to budget constraints over the past decade.

[19]The three U.S. representatives serve on both JEMCO and JEMFAC and include one official each from Interior, State, and HHS, with the Interior representative serving as Chairman of both oversight bodies. A revision, under preparation since 2003, to a 1986 executive order outlining specific responsibilities of the U.S. agencies regarding compact matters had not been issued as of June 2013, according to Interior officials.

under the compacts. JEMCO's and JEMFAC's designated roles and responsibilities include the following:

- reviewing the budget and development plans from each of the governments;
- approving grant allocations and performance objectives;[20]
- attaching terms and conditions to any or all annual grant awards to improve program performance and fiscal accountability;
- evaluating progress, management problems, and any shifts in priorities in each sector; and
- reviewing audits called for in the compacts.

In practice, JEMCO and JEMFAC allocate grants and attach terms and conditions to grant awards through resolutions, which are discussed and voted upon at their meetings.

From fiscal years 2004 through 2013, JEMCO and JEMFAC allocated about $1.1 billion in sector grants to the FSM and RMI under the amended compacts. In practice, JEMFAC has allocated Ebeye special needs funds as a separate grant allocation, resulting in seven sectors. For more detailed information on compact sector allocations, see appendix V.

FSM and RMI Grant Administration

The FSM national and state governments and the RMI government are to manage the sector and supplemental education grants and monitor day-to-day operations to ensure compliance with grant terms and conditions. The governments are also required to track progress toward performance goals and report quarterly to the United States. The FSM and the RMI must annually report to the U.S. President on the use of U.S. grant assistance and other U.S. assistance provided during the prior fiscal year, and must also report on their progress in meeting program and economic

[20] JEMCO and JEMFAC render decisions by majority vote, except those decisions regarding the division of RMI grants among sectors, which are made by consensus. JEMCO and JEMFAC are also responsible for approving the plans that form the basis for the use of the supplemental education grants annually. The U.S. appointees to JEMCO and JEMFAC are required by the compacts' implementing legislation to "consult with the Secretary of Education regarding the objectives, use, and monitoring of United States financial, program, and technical assistance made available for educational purposes." (Pub. L. No. 108-188, §105(f)(1)(B)(i), Dec. 17, 2003).

goals.[21] Each country has established an agency dedicated to providing compact oversight and ensuring compliance with regulations in the amended compacts, grant award terms and conditions, and JEMCO and JEMFAC resolutions.

The FSM and the RMI must adhere to specific fiscal control and accounting procedures and are required to submit annual audit reports, within the meaning of the Single Audit Act, as amended.[22] Single audits are focused on recipients' internal controls over financial reporting and compliance with laws and regulations governing U.S. federal awardees and provide key information about the federal grantee's financial management and reporting.

U.S. Grant Administration

Through its participation in the JEMCO and JEMFAC, the United States can require that terms and conditions be attached to any and all annual grant awards to improve program performance and fiscal accountability. Interior's Office of Insular Affairs (OIA) has responsibility for the administration and oversight of the FSM and RMI compact sector and supplemental education grants.[23] In addition to headquarters staff, OIA operates a Honolulu field office and has staff in the FSM and RMI to

---

[21]According to an official with Interior's Office of Insular Affairs (OIA), the FSM and the RMI have not fulfilled their annual reporting requirements from fiscal years 2004 through 2012. Both FSM and RMI officials expressed their concerns with the annual report due date because it conflicts with the preparation and availability of other reports that are needed to complete the annual report.

[22]31 U.S.C. § 7501 et seq. According to the act, single audit reports are due to the Federal Audit Clearinghouse within 9 months after the end of the audited period. OIA uses the date of filing with the clearinghouse to determine when the country has completed the audit process.

[23]Under the amended compacts' implementing legislation, the U.S. President is required to report annually to Congress on the use and effectiveness of U.S. assistance. The President's report is also to include an assessment of U.S. program and technical assistance provided to the countries and an evaluation of their economic conditions. OIA officials told us they assist in drafting these annual reports, which were issued in 2004 through 2011. Additionally, during the year of the 5th, 10th and 15th anniversaries of the enactments of the law, the annual reports should include a review of the terms of the respective compacts and consider the overall nature and development of the U.S.–FSM and U.S.–RMI relationships. The United States issued 5-year reviews of the FSM and RMI in 2012.

conduct oversight.[24] Under the fiscal procedures agreements governing the amended compacts, OIA is responsible for using financial reports to monitor each country's budget and fiscal performance, and for using performance reports submitted by the countries to evaluate sector grant performance. OIA officials are also responsible for monitoring compliance with grant terms and conditions. If problems are found in areas such as the FSM and RMI monitoring of sector grants or a lack of compliance with grant terms, the United States may impose special conditions or restrictions, including requiring the acquisition of technical or management assistance, requiring additional reporting and monitoring, or requiring additional prior approvals. Additionally, the United States may withhold grant funds if the countries breach the terms and conditions of certain sections of the amended compacts or of the fiscal procedures agreements, or fail to comply with the award conditions of a grant.

As the U.S. agency with the largest grant awards to the FSM and the RMI, Interior is designated as the cognizant audit agency[25] for FSM and RMI single audits and has several responsibilities, including

- providing technical advice to auditees and auditors and considering grant extensions to the report submission date,
- informing other affected federal agencies of any direct reporting of irregularities or illegal acts, and
- coordinating the federal response for audit findings that affect the federal program of more than one agency.[26]

---

[24]The amended compacts' implementing legislation states that "it is the sense of Congress that the Secretary of the Interior shall ensure that there are personnel resources committed in the appropriate numbers and locations to ensure effective oversight of U.S. assistance." See Pub. L. No. 108-188, §105(b)(8).

[25]The cognizant agency is the federal agency designated to carry out the federal responsbilities with regard to a single audit and is the agency that provides the predominant amount of direct funding to an entity, such as the FSM and the RMI. Grantees receiving more than $50 million in federal assistance are assigned to a cognizant agency for audit supervision. See Office of Management and Budget, *Audits of States, Local Governments, and Non-Profit Organizations*, OMB Circular No. A-133 (revised 2007).

[26]This coordinated federal response is the "management decision" for audit findings. Management decision means the evaluation by the federal awarding agency of audit findings and corrective action plan and the issuance of a written decision as to what corrective action is necessary.

Furthermore, all U.S. agencies providing noncompact grants to the FSM and the RMI are responsible for administering those grants in accordance with Office of Management and Budget (OMB) requirements[27] and agency regulations that include the Grants Management Common Rule. Under the common rule, U.S. agencies may consider a grantee as "high risk" if the grantee has a history of unsatisfactory performance, is not financially stable, has a management system that does not meet required standards, has not conformed to the terms and conditions of previous awards, or is otherwise irresponsible. Single audits provide key information about the adequacy of a grantee's management system. Federal agencies that designate a grantee as high risk may impose special grant conditions.[28]

FSM and RMI Spending Targeted Education and Health

In fiscal years 2007 through 2011, the FSM and RMI spent at least half of their compact sector funds in the education and health sectors. Most of the compact funds in these sectors paid for personnel costs and medical supplies and equipment. Both countries spent significant amounts of compact funds on personnel in the education and health sectors, which resulted in JEMCO and JEMFAC resolutions aimed at capping the budgetary levels for personnel in these sectors at fiscal year 2011 levels because of concerns about the sustainability of sector budgets as compact funding continues to decline through fiscal year 2023. While the four FSM states completed plans in 2012 and 2013 to address the annual decrements in compact sector funding through fiscal year 2023, the FSM National Government and the RMI have not submitted plans to address the decrements. As a result, the U.S. members of the JEMCO and JEMFAC are considering withholding certain fiscal year 2014 compact sector grant funds until the FSM National Government and RMI submit their plans. At the annual JEMCO and JEMFAC meetings in August 2013,

---

[27] See Office of Management and Budget, *Grants and Cooperative Agreements with State and Local Governments*, OMB Circular No. A-102 (revised 1997).

[28] According to the grants management common rule, a high-risk designation is authorized if a grantee has a history of unsatisfactory performance or otherwise irresponsible actions, such as failing to submit single audit reports in a timely manner or if single audits or other Inspector General investigations reveal substantial and pervasive problems. Such a designation allows the grantor to impose special terms and conditions or sanctions that could result in suspensions or terminations of federal awards. The grants management common rule was established in 1987 under presidential direction to adopt government-wide terms and conditions for grants to state and local governments. Each federal department incorporates the rule in its agency regulations.

fiscal year 2014 sector grant funds were not allocated to the FSM or the RMI.

FSM Sector Expenditures

FSM Spent Most Compact Funds in Education and Health, and Personnel Costs Were the Largest Component

In fiscal years 2007 through 2011, the FSM spent about 67 percent, or $158 million, of sector compact funds in the education and health sectors.[29] As seen in figure 3, of the total expenditures in all six compact sectors, expenditures for education represented approximately 37 percent and expenditures for health represented about 30 percent. Expenditures in the other four sectors—infrastructure, environment, private sector development, and public sector capacity building—together accounted for about 33 percent of total compact expenditures during this period. In addition to education sector compact funds, the FSM also spent about $35.7 million in supplemental education grant funds to support education initiatives. For information on FSM infrastructure sector compact expenditures, see appendix II.

Figure 3: Federated States of Micronesia (FSM) Sector Compact Expenditures and Supplemental Education Grant Expenditures, Fiscal Years 2007 through 2011

FSM sector compact and supplemental education grant expenditures (dollars in millions)

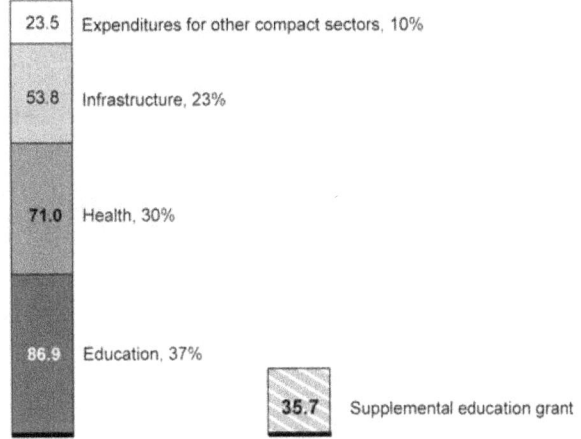

23.5	Expenditures for other compact sectors, 10%
53.8	Infrastructure, 23%
71.0	Health, 30%
86.9	Education, 37%
35.7	Supplemental education grant

Sources: GAO analysis based on information from FSM National Government, Chuuk, and Pohnpei single audit reports.

[29]Since we focused our review on the FSM National Government and the state governments of Chuuk and Pohnpei, the FSM expenditure amount includes data for these three governments. Data for the state governments of Kosrae and Yap are not included.

Compact funds in the FSM supported a significant portion of government expenditures in the education and health sectors. Education sector compact and supplemental education grant funds together constituted about 85 percent of total education expenditures, and health sector compact funds constituted about 66 percent of total health expenditures in fiscal year 2011.[30] Other noncompact U.S. grants represented an additional 10 percent of the education expenditures and 25 percent of health expenditures in fiscal year 2011.

With regard to the use of funds, in fiscal years 2009 through 2011, the FSM spent about 61 percent of its education sector compact and supplemental education grant funds to pay personnel, and about 41 percent of its health sector compact funds to pay personnel (see fig. 4).

---

[30]The reliance on compact funds as sources of government expenditures varies among the FSM governments, with education sector compact and supplemental education grant expenditures together accounting for almost 20 percent of total education expenditures in the National Government, 100 percent in Chuuk, and 91 percent in Pohnpei, according to data from the 2011 single audits. Health sector compact funds accounted for about 9 percent of total health expenditures in the National Government, 98 percent in Chuuk, and 72 percent in Pohnpei.

Figure 4: Federated States of Micronesia (FSM) Compact Expenditures in the Education and Health Sectors, Fiscal Years 2009 through 2011

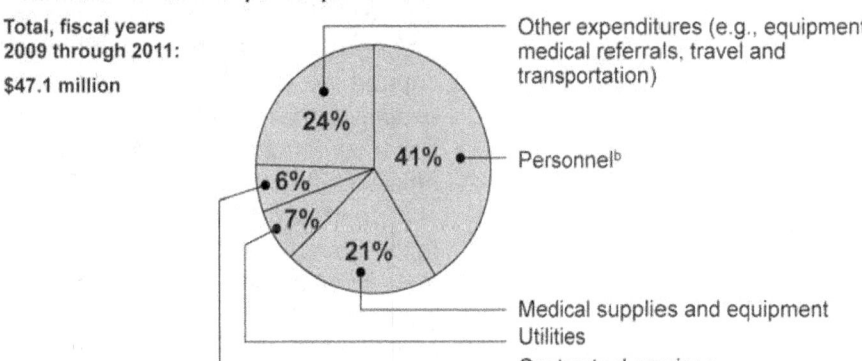

FSM education sector compact expenditures[a]

Total, fiscal years 2009 through 2011:

$78.1 million

Other expenditures (e.g., books and instructional supplies, food stuffs, travel and transportation)

24%

5%
5%
6%

61% Personnel[b]

Scholarships and allowances
Contractual services
Office supplies and materials

FSM health sector compact expenditures

Total, fiscal years 2009 through 2011:

$47.1 million

Other expenditures (e.g., equipment, medical referrals, travel and transportation)

24%

6%
7%
21%

41% Personnel[b]

Medical supplies and equipment
Utilities
Contractual services

Sources: GAO analysis based on information from FSM National Government, Chuuk, and Pohnpei single audit reports.

Notes: Percentages may not add up to 100 due to rounding. Because specific expenditure data for the FSM National Government and Chuuk were not presented in their single audits for fiscal years 2007 and 2008, we only present specific expenditures for the three entities for fiscal years 2009 through 2011.

[a]Includes both education sector compact and supplemental education grant expenditures.

[b]Includes categories defined as regular wages, overtime, fringe benefits, and other personnel costs.

The levels of expenditures in the FSM education and health sectors dedicated to personnel concerned JEMCO because of the potential effects on the sustainability of sector budgets as compact funding continued to decline through fiscal year 2023 because of the annual decrements. In September 2011, JEMCO resolved that it would not approve fiscal year 2013 budgets for the education and health sectors until the FSM demonstrated that budgetary levels for personnel expenses reflected in education and health sector proposals did not exceed fiscal year 2011 levels.[31] According to OIA, the FSM complied with this resolution in its fiscal year 2013 compact funding proposals.

The Four FSM States Completed Plans to Address the Annual Decrements through 2023, but FSM National Government Lacks a Plan

In March 2013, the four FSM states had completed plans to address the annual decreases, or decrements, in compact sector funding through 2023; however, the FSM National Government has not completed a plan to address the fiscal challenges facing the government because of the annual decrements. The states' plans, completed in 2012 and early 2013, detail the proposed expenditure cuts across sector budgets intended to offset the annual decrements while preserving essential services in the education and health sectors. Absent additional revenues, proposed cuts are to be implemented in 2014, 2017, and 2020.

While U.S. JEMCO members expressed their satisfaction with the FSM states' plans, at the March 2013 JEMCO midyear meeting, they called for the FSM National Government to create a plan addressing how it will manage the fiscal challenges facing the government and how it will support the states in managing annual decrements.[32] An FSM official explained that the FSM National Government did not create a plan because it receives only a small portion of FSM compact funds. The official said the FSM National Government was focused instead on shifting its sector operating costs, such as for the College of Micronesia, to the government's own funds, freeing up compact funds for priorities in the education and health sectors. The FSM official also noted the government's efforts to develop an operational plan by early 2014 outlining how the FSM government will address the budgetary and economic challenges it faces through 2023 and beyond. In May 2013, the three U.S. JEMCO members notified the FSM that the United States was

---

[31]JEMCO resolution 2011-1.

[32]U.S. officials called for this plan on the basis of two prior JEMCO resolutions related to annual decrement planning: JEMCO resolution 2009-2 and JEMCO resolution 2010-2. JEMCO resolution 2009-2 called for the FSM national and state governments to develop plans for managing the annual decrements in compact funding and use those plans as the basis for its fiscal year 2012 budget decisions. Because the FSM did not submit national or state plans prior to an August 10, 2010, deadline, JEMCO resolution 2010-2 called for a report addressing a variety of issues relating to long-term sustainability, such as the need to constrain expenditures, increase revenues, and find additional contributors to increase compact trust fund annual contributions in order to adjust to projected budget levels after fiscal year 2023.

GAO-13-675 Compacts of Free Association

considering withholding select fiscal year 2014 compact sector funds from the FSM National Government until it completes a plan detailing the concrete commitments that will be made to complement and support the states' plans to address the annual decrements in compact sector funding. Without this plan, the FSM may not be able to sustain essential services in the education and health sectors in the absence of compact funding. The FSM National Government responded in July 2013 indicating that to address the decrement it was considering, among other things, tax reform, alternative energy initiatives, an annual funding set-aside, increased FSM trust fund contributions, and improved revenue sharing with the states. In its comments on our draft report, the FSM National Government mentioned the issue of revenue sharing between the national and state governments, noting that the FSM leadership is working together to arrive at a decision that will be beneficial to both levels of government and at the same time facilitate greater effectiveness in meeting the development objectives of the FSM. (See app. X for a copy of the FSM's comments.) At the annual JEMCO meeting in August 2013, fiscal year 2014 sector grant funds were not allocated to the FSM.

RMI Sector Expenditures

RMI Spent Half of Compact Funds in Education and Health, and Personnel Costs Were the Largest Component

In fiscal years 2007 through 2011, the RMI spent about 50 percent, or $89 million, of sector compact funds in the education and health sectors. As shown in figure 5, of the total compact expenditures within the seven compact sectors (including Ebeye special needs as a sector), education represented approximately 31 percent and health represented approximately 19 percent. Expenditures in the other five sectors—infrastructure, environment, private sector development, public sector capacity building, and Ebeye special needs—together accounted for about 50 percent of total compact expenditures during this period. In addition to education sector compact funds, the RMI spent about $26.5 million of supplemental education grant funds and $11.9 million of Ebeye special needs funds to support education initiatives. In addition to health sector compact funds, the RMI spent about $3 million of Ebeye special needs funds to support health initiatives. For information on RMI infrastructure sector compact expenditures, see appendix II.

Figure 5: Republic of the Marshall Islands (RMI) Sector Compact Expenditures and Supplemental Education Grant Expenditures, Fiscal Years 2007 through 2011

RMI sector compact and supplemental education grant expenditures (dollars in millions)

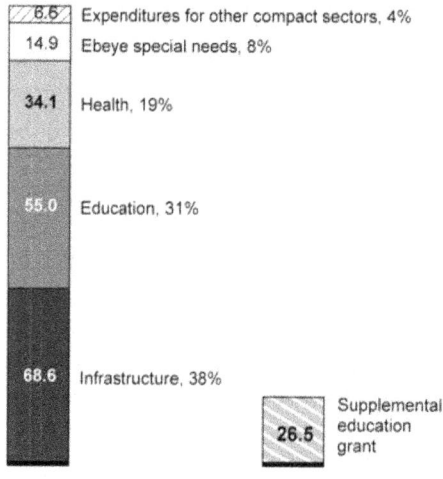

Sources: GAO analysis based on information from RMI single audit reports.

Compact funds in the RMI supported a significant portion of government expenditures in the education and health sectors. Education sector compact funds, supplemental education grants, and Ebeye special needs education funds constituted about 62 percent of total education expenditures in fiscal year 2011, while health sector compact funds and Ebeye special needs health funds constituted about 33 percent of total health expenditures. Other noncompact U.S. grants represented an additional 6 percent of education expenditures and 17 percent of health expenditures in fiscal year 2011.

In fiscal years 2007 through 2011, the RMI spent most education and health compact funds on personnel: about 54 percent of the education sector compact and supplemental education grant funds paid for personnel, while about 64 percent of the health sector compact funds paid for personnel (see fig. 6).

Figure 6: Republic of the Marshall Islands (RMI) Compact Expenditures in the Education and Health Sectors, Fiscal Years 2007 through 2011

RMI education sector compact expenditures[a]

Total, fiscal years 2007 through 2011:

$81.5 million

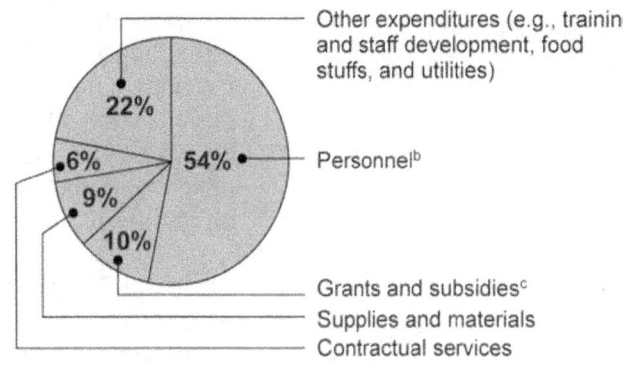

Other expenditures (e.g., training and staff development, food stuffs, and utilities)

22%

6%

54% — Personnel[b]

9%

10%

Grants and subsidies[c]

Supplies and materials

Contractual services

RMI health sector compact expenditures

Total, fiscal years 2007 through 2011:

$34.1 million

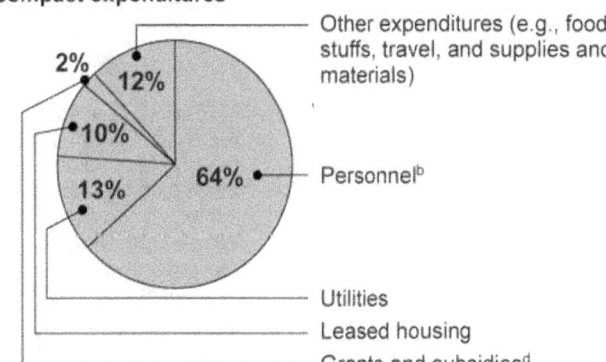

Other expenditures (e.g., food stuffs, travel, and supplies and materials)

2%   12%

10%

13%   64% — Personnel[b]

Utilities

Leased housing

Grants and subsidies[d]

Sources: GAO analysis based on information from RMI single audit reports.

Notes: Percentages may not add up to 100 due to rounding. This figure does not include an analysis of Ebeye special needs expenditures.

[a]Includes both education sector compact and supplemental education grant expenditures.

[b]Includes salaries and wages.

[c]Represents payments in aid to nonpublic schools and transfers out to the College of Micronesia.

[d]Represents payments made to the Majuro Atoll Waste Company in accordance with grant agreements.

Due to interrelated concerns about the amount of funds dedicated to personnel costs and the sustainability of sector budgets, JEMFAC resolved in August 2011 that personnel-related expenses in the education and health sector budgets for fiscal year 2012 could not exceed fiscal year 2011 levels and directed that fiscal year 2012 compact funds made available by this change should be budgeted for direct support of education and health programs and services.[33] According to OIA, the RMI complied with this resolution.

RMI Has Not Updated Its Plan to Address Annual Decrements in Compact Funding

The RMI has not updated its plan to address the annual decrements in compact funding.[34] In March 2011, the RMI submitted a draft medium-term budget and investment framework, which included a plan to address the annual decrements and provided an overview of economic performance, the country's fiscal situation, and budget estimates.[35] However, U.S. JEMFAC members raised concerns that the framework did not account for significant ongoing health sector operational costs, relied on reform efforts, and assumed unlikely new revenues.

While the RMI provided a draft update to its framework in July 2013,[36] the government has not updated the plan for addressing the annual decrements. The RMI budget submissions for fiscal years 2012 and 2013

---

[33] JEMFAC resolution 2011-1.

[34] JEMFAC passed two resolutions related to annual decrement planning: JEMFAC resolution 2009-1 and JEMFAC resolution 2010-1. JEMFAC resolution 2009-1 called for the RMI to develop plans for managing annual decreases in compact funding and use those plans as the basis for fiscal year 2012 budget decisions. Because the RMI did not submit plans prior to an August 10, 2010, deadline, JEMFAC passed another resolution in 2010— JEMFAC resolution 2010-1— that called for a report addressing a variety of issues relating to the RMI's fiscal challenges, such as the need to make adjustments to take into account the effect of the decrement in the medium term.

[35] In 2006, we reported that the FSM and RMI lacked concrete plans for addressing the annual decrements in compact funding and would likely be unable to sustain current levels of government services as compact funding diminishes. We recommended that Interior, in conjunction with JEMCO, JEMFAC, and other U.S. agencies, work with the FSM and the RMI to establish plans for sector spending and investment to minimize any adverse consequence of reduced funding. See GAO-07-163. While the FSM and the RMI provided draft annual decrement plans to the JEMCO and JEMFAC in 2011, JEMCO challenged the viability of the FSM National Government's decrement strategy, and JEMFAC advised the RMI government to extend its decrement strategy beyond the medium term to mitigate the elimination of compact funding in 2023.

[36] According to the U.S.–RMI amended compact implementing legislation, "the Government of the Republic of the Marshall Islands shall prepare and maintain an official medium-term budget and investment framework. The framework shall be strategic in nature, shall be continuously reviewed and updated through the annual budget process, and shall make projections on a multi-year rolling basis" (Pub. L. No. 108-188, §201(b), §211(f)). According to Article V of the fiscal procedures agreement, U.S. grant assistance shall be made available in accordance with annually updated implementation steps for the medium-term budget and investment framework, developed by the RMI in conjunction with its budget process.

did not reflect the RMI's commitments outlined in the framework and failed to address JEMFAC's ongoing concerns regarding decrement planning. An RMI official responded that the RMI government could not provide the updated framework and annual decrement plan because of obstacles it encountered in completing the 2011 audit and finalizing the 2011 census. In April 2013, the three U.S. JEMFAC members notified the RMI that the United States was considering withholding fiscal year 2014 compact sector funds from the RMI until the RMI submits the framework and an annual decrement plan. In July 2013, RMI officials submitted an updated framework outlining anticipated revenues in the medium term, but it lacked an annual decrement plan, as required. Without the annual decrement plan, the RMI may not be able to sustain essential services in the education and health sectors in the medium term. At the August 2013 JEMFAC meeting, the RMI submitted an updated medium-term budget and investment framework dated August 2013 along with several budget portfolio statements for fiscal year 2014 including statements for the departments of health and education. The RMI government considers this to be its decrement plan. However, the information was provided to the U.S. members of the JEMFAC 3 days prior to the annual meeting, and according to these members, they did not have sufficient time to review it and determine whether or not it meets the requirements of the JEMFAC resolution. At the annual JEMFAC meeting in August 2013, fiscal year 2014 sector grant funds were not allocated to the RMI.

Data Inconsistencies Hindered Our Assessment of FSM and RMI Progress in the Education and Health Sectors

Data reliability issues hindered our assessment of progress by the FSM and RMI in both the education and health sectors for fiscal years 2007 through 2011. Between 2004 and 2006, both countries began tracking education and health indicators, establishing data collection systems, and collecting data for the majority of the indicators and have continued to track data on their indicators since that time. (See app. VI for a list of all FSM and RMI indicators in the education and health sectors.) While both countries tracked annual indicators to measure progress in these sectors, in reviewing subsets of these indicators we determined that data for eight of the subset of nine education indicators we reviewed in the FSM and for three of the subset of five education indicators we reviewed in the RMI were not sufficiently reliable to assess progress for the compacts as a whole—for a variety of reasons, some specific to individual indicators, but primarily because of missing, incomplete, or inconsistent data. We found one RMI education indicator to be both reliable and capable of demonstrating progress: the education level of teachers in the RMI. The other reliable RMI education indicator was student enrollment. We determined that data for all five of the subset of FSM health indicators we reviewed were not sufficiently reliable to assess progress for the compacts as a whole. In the RMI, of the subset of five health indicators we reviewed, we determined that one was sufficiently reliable and two were not sufficiently reliable to assess progress; for the remaining two indicators, we had no basis to judge the reliability of the data. In much of their reporting on these indicators, the FSM and RMI have noted data reliability problems and some actions they have taken to address the problems. The compacts' joint management and accountability committees have also raised concerns about the reliability of the FSM's education and health data and the RMI's health data and required that each country obtain an independent assessment and verification of these data; neither country has met that requirement.

Assessment of FSM Progress in Education

FSM Has Tracked Annual Indicators in Education since 2005, but We Found Problems with Data Reliability

In 2004, the FSM established 20 indicators to track progress toward its overarching goals in education:[37] to improve the educational system of the country, including primary, secondary, and postsecondary education, and to develop the country's human and material resources necessary to deliver these services. However, our review of a subset of 9 of the 20 FSM education indicators found problems with data reliability. Table 1 provides a summary of the data reliability determinations we made in reviewing the subset of 9 education indicators. (For a complete list of the indicators the FSM has tracked and reported since fiscal year 2005, see app. VI.)

---

[37]This came in response to a 2004 JEMCO resolution requesting that the FSM National Government and the four state Departments of Education reconfirm the goals that would be tracked uniformly and consistently beginning in fiscal year 2005, to enable reporting of results and make comparisons possible over time and across states.

Table 1: Subset of 9 of the 20 Federated States of Micronesia (FSM) Education Indicators Reviewed, with Observations on the Reliability of the Data to Measure Progress for the Compact as a Whole from 2007 through 2011

Indicator	Observations on data reliability	Sufficiently reliable to measure progress over time? Yes, No, or No basis to judge
Student enrollment	Inconsistent inclusion of private school enrollment data among FSM states.	No
8th and 12th grade completion/graduation rate	Incomplete data among FSM states.	No
Number of schools by grade level		Yes
Education level of staff	Inconsistent inclusion of private school staff information among FSM states.	No
Dropout rate	Inconsistent definitions and data collection between FSM states.	No
Students at "Proficiency" level or above on standardized tests	Data missing for some FSM states; no individual state reporting for some years; and in some years and for some grades less than half the students in the grades were tested.	No
Teacher attendance	Concern about reliability of school sourced documents.	No
Parent involvement	Incomplete data and inconsistent definitions among FSM states.	No
Scholarships	Inconsistent reporting of required information among FSM states.	No

Source: GAO analysis of FSM data

Notes: By "sufficiently reliable," we mean that the likelihood of significant errors or incompleteness is minimal, and the use of the data would not lead to an incorrect or unintentional message. The indicator titles are shortened in the table; for the full indicator titles, see app. VI.

We determined that the data for number of schools by grade level were sufficiently reliable to report on progress in the FSM education sector. The number of schools by grade level, by itself, does not necessarily demonstrate progress or lack thereof; however, it does provide useful information about the changes in the states' education systems. Both Chuuk and Pohnpei, for example, have gone through a process resulting in school closures, with or without consolidation of some schools, and the numbers of schools by grade level reflect this. In Chuuk, the number of schools declined from a total of 154 primary and secondary schools in 2007 to 85 schools in 2012, a 45 percent reduction.[38] In Pohnpei, the

---

[38]The consolidation included the merger of 46 early childhood education centers with elementary schools, as well as the merging of 22 elementary schools with other schools in close proximity.

number of schools declined from a total of 41 primary and secondary schools in 2007 to 34 schools in 2011, a 17 percent reduction.

We determined that 8 of the subset of 9 FSM education indicators we reviewed could not be used to assess progress over time because of data reliability issues summarized above in table 1. For example, we found that the four FSM states did not use common definitions for some indicators; consequently, the education indicator reports we reviewed do not contain consistent data for these indicators and comparisons cannot be made across states. As an example, Chuuk, Pohnpei, and the FSM National Government each applied its own definition of dropout, creating inconsistencies in the data for that indicator.[39] Student enrollment data provide another example: Chuuk and Kosrae included both public and private schools in reporting student enrollment data, while Pohnpei and Yap included only public schools. In addition to data reporting inconsistencies, we found that data in FSM's education indicators reports sometimes were not complete. For example, in 2011, average daily student attendance data for Chuuk were missing; for that same year, Chuuk also lacked completion and graduation rate data for 8th and 12th graders.

Site-Visit Observations Relating to Progress in the FSM Education Sector

During January 2013 site visits in Chuuk, we visited 13 school sites selected on the basis of available time and travel constraints. This included 6 of 8 schools on the island of Weno and 7 schools on four lagoon islands.[40] In several cases, these were school sites we visited in 2006. In facilities we were able to visit both in 2006 and 2013, we noted general improvements in the overall maintenance and condition; however,

---

[39]The FSM National Government considered students to be dropouts if they had not come to school for 40 days and had not requested a transcript. In Chuuk, an education official stated that elementary students with an individualized education program who missed 15 consecutive days were considered dropouts, whereas high school students who had 5 days of unexcused absence were considered dropouts. The Pohnpei Department of Education did not have a definition for when a student is considered a dropout; but noted it collected dropout data only for high school students, not for elementary students. According to the *FSM JEMCO 20 Education Indicators Report, July 2007*, the definition of "dropout" was revisited in a May 2007 data management workshop. Participants agreed that a completely reliable definition was probably unattainable, though it was stressed to participants that simply subtracting ending enrollment from beginning enrollment, which at least two states had done, was not a reliable method to calculate the dropout rate.

[40]The site visits we made in Chuuk and Pohnpei were intended to illustrate educational conditions in those states. Our observations are not generalizable to the other states or to the FSM as a whole.

staff we interviewed reported that a lack of chairs, desks, and textbooks was a concern, especially in lagoon-island schools. In addition, we visited the Chuuk Department of Education warehouse where we found hundreds of cases of books and supplies that had not been shipped to schools in the outer islands as intended, according to the warehouse manager. An OIA education grant manager reported that the department had recently purchased and distributed 4,000 chairs and the distribution process had gone smoothly.[41] However, as of May 2013, Chuuk did not have a fully implemented purchasing plan, inventory management system, or monitoring plan for textbooks, as required by JEMCO, according to an OIA official.

In Pohnpei, we visited 8 schools (5 elementary and 3 high schools) of a total of 34 public elementary and high schools on the main island of Pohnpei, selected on the basis of available time and travel constraints. The school buildings we visited were generally clean. From what we were able to observe, they had electricity, functioning fans in the classrooms, and functioning windows. We observed desks, chairs, and textbooks in the classrooms. The newly built schools that we visited, which were funded through public sector infrastructure grants, had water tanks and new bathrooms with sinks and toilets that appeared to be operational. From what we observed, these schools were generally maintained in good condition. However, we also noted minor issues such as chipped paint and broken classroom doors and locks in some facilities.

Assessment of FSM Progress in Health

FSM Has Tracked Annual Indicators in Health since 2004, but We Found Problems with Data Reliability

In 2004, the FSM began tracking data on 14 health indicators to measure its progress toward improving diagnostic and treatment capacity and ensuring the provision of services to geographically dispersed populations (see app. VI for a complete list of the indicators). However, our review of a subset of 5 of the 14 FSM health indicators found problems with data

---

[41]A 2009 FSM National Government audit report covering fiscal years 2006 and 2007 also found that some textbooks had been sitting in Chuuk's warehouse for up to 8 months. See Federated States of Micronesia, Office of the National Public Auditor, *Inspection of Procurement Activities at Chuuk Department of Education, FY2006-2007,* Report No. 2009-02 (Palikir, Pohnpei: July 2009). Similar problems existed in 2006 when we visited. See GAO, *Compacts of Free Association: Micronesia's and the Marshall Islands' Use of Sector Grants,* GAO-07-514R (Washington, D.C.: May 25, 2007).

reliability. We determined that none of these indicators could be used to assess progress because of data reliability issues (see table 2).

Table 2: Subset of 5 of the 14 Federated States of Micronesia (FSM) Health Indicators Reviewed, with Observations on the Reliability of the Data to Measure Progress for the Compact as a Whole from 2007 through 2011

Indicator	Observations on data reliability	Sufficiently reliable to measure progress over time? Yes, No, or No basis to judge
Infant mortality rate	Underreported births and deaths, and lack of outer island data.	No
Immunization coverage (2-year olds)	Unreliable data in one FSM state.	No
Off-island medical referral costs	Source of expenditure data upon which assessments were based is unclear.	No
Essential drugs	Unreliable inventory records.	No
Diabetes-related hospitalizations	Discrepancies in reported data.	No

Source: GAO analysis of FSM health indicator data for 2007-2011.

Notes: By "sufficiently reliable," we mean that the likelihood of significant errors or incompleteness is minimal, and the use of the data would not lead to an incorrect or unintentional message. The indicator titles are shortened in the table; for the full indicator titles, see app. VI.

We found inconsistencies in the data provided by the states compared with data for the same indicators included in the FSM's 14 annual health indicators report. For example, FSM data on immunization cannot be used due to issues with data in Chuuk. According to the FSM immunization expert, the data for that indicator were unreliable prior to 2011 because in Chuuk there was no registry of immunization to allow the computation of a coverage rate. In reviewing the Chuuk medical records, the immunization expert found that (1) an individual child might have three different immunization records in the system under three variations of his or her name, and (2) there was not appropriate consideration as to when a vaccination was medically valid and therefore should be counted. For an immunization to be medically valid, for example, a series may need to be given within certain time frames. The records that the expert examined showed vaccinations being given too early in the sequence, resulting in an incorrect dosage and invalidating the vaccination. Finally, the expert noted that immunization program documentation was bad. We also identified problems when reviewing how the FSM calculates the percentage of days when all essential drugs are in stock. Specifically, we identified problems with the source documents used in the calculations in Chuuk and Pohnpei, calling into question the reliability of the data presented in the health indicators report. The key documents from each health care facility that are used to calculate the indicator are the formulary (the list of the essential drugs) and each facility's inventory report. We attempted to verify the accuracy of the Chuuk hospital drug inventory report and found that the report contained some incorrect information. For example, the report listed 219 bottles of Amoxicillin 125 MG/5ML Suspension 150 ML, but the hospital's storage room had none. Since the inventory report is used in calculating the number reported for the essential drugs indicator, incorrect information found in the report raises questions about the validity and reliability of the information for this indicator in the health indicators report.

Site-Visit Observations Relating to Progress in the FSM Health Sector

In January 2013, we visited Chuuk's only hospital, which we had previously visited in 2006. We noted that the hospital was generally better maintained than it had been on our prior visit. Moreover, officials told us that it now has reliable and consistent electric power, which was not the case in the past. Additionally, whereas previously Chuuk's hospital had only a small incinerator to burn medical waste, we observed two functioning medical waste incinerators, which we were told operate on a routine basis. In 2006, some of the selected medical equipment that we observed was not working. In 2013, the selected equipment that we observed, such as a digital X-ray machine and laboratory equipment, was being used and reported as functional.

During our 2006 visit to Chuuk's hospital, many of the on-hand drugs that we spot checked were past their expiration days. On our 2013 visit to the hospital, however, the majority of the on-hand drugs that we spot-checked were within their labeled expiration dates. We also spot-checked drugs in two dispensaries on Chuuk Lagoon islands and found most of the drugs we checked to be within their labeled expiration dates. We cannot comment regarding on-hand drugs at the three other dispensaries in Chuuk lagoon that we visited, as they were closed when we attempted to visit them even though their schedules indicated that they were supposed to be open.[42]

During our 2006 visit to selected Pohnpei dispensaries, we also had found that varying amounts of the drugs on hand that we spot checked were past their expiration dates. On our recent visit to three of the four dispensaries on the main island, however, most of the on-hand drugs that

---

[42]The closed dispensaries were the Parem Island dispensary, Tonoas's Sapun dispensary, and Fefen's Sapore dispensary. The open dispensaries were Udot's Funomo dispensary and Fefen's Messa dispensary.

we spot checked in selected dispensaries were within their expiration dates or had an extended shelf life.[43]

The three dispensary buildings we selected on Pohnpei in 2013 were all open on the day we visited. In addition, health assistants were present at the time of our visits. The buildings all generally appeared to be in an acceptable condition and had electricity at the time of our visits. The three selected dispensaries also reported some concerns, however. For example, we found some equipment, such as scales and freezers that were not functioning at the time of our visit. We also visited Pohnpei's only public hospital during our site visits. However major renovation work was taking place on the day of our visit, which made it impossible to make any observations about its normal functioning. (For information on compact-funded infrastructure projects in the education and health sectors, see app. II.)

Assessment of RMI Progress in Education

RMI Has Tracked Annual Indicators in Education since 2004, but We Found Problems with Data Reliability

The RMI has tracked 20 indicators selected by JEMFAC in 2004 for monitoring progress in education and began reporting on them annually in 2005 in response to a JEMFAC resolution.[44] The RMI's overarching education goals were to improve the educational system of the country, including primary, secondary, and postsecondary education, and to develop the country's human and material resources necessary to deliver these services. For a complete list of the indicators the RMI has tracked and reported from 2007 through 2011, see appendix VI.

However, in our review of a subset of 5 of the 20 RMI education indicators, we found problems with data reliability (see table 3).

---

[43]The spot checks we performed were intended to provide insights into whether drugs were past their expiry dates. Our observations are not generalizable to all drugs in Chuuk and Pohnpei.

[44]In 2004, the first year of the amended compact, the requirement was to submit quarterly performance reports with the 20 uniform indicators of education progress. The 2005 JEMFAC resolution required the RMI to report annually on the 20 indicators.

Table 3: Subset of 5 of the 20 Republic of the Marshall Islands (RMI) Education Indicators Reviewed, with Observations on the Reliability of the Data to Measure Progress for the Compact as a Whole from 2007 through 2011

Indicator	Observations on data reliability	Sufficiently reliable to measure progress over time? Yes, No, or No basis to judge
Student enrollment		Yes
Completion/graduation rate	Revision to data with no explanation; officials raised concerns about the reliability of the data.	No
Education level of staff		Yes
Dropout rate	Lack of outer island data; missing data.	No
Students at "Proficiency" level or above on standardized tests	Inconsistency in reported data for some years; number of students tested also unknown.	No

Source: GAO analysis of RMI data.

Notes: We considered the data for education level of staff to be sufficiently reliable for school years 2008-2009 through 2011-2012 but not for 2007-2008. We excluded school year 2007-2008 because the RMI included private school teachers in these data and did not explain its inclusion, whereas in all other years the RMI is clear the data represent only public school teachers. By "sufficiently reliable," we mean that the likelihood of significant errors or incompleteness is minimal, and the use of the data would not lead to an incorrect or unintentional message. The indicator titles are shortened in the table; for the full indicator titles, see app. VI.

We determined that the data for 2 indicators were sufficiently reliable to assess progress in the RMI's education sector: (1) total enrollment by grade and gender and (2) number and percentage of teachers by education level. Data we reviewed showed an improvement in the qualifications of RMI teaching staff, with the percentage of teachers having no degree, or a high school diploma, or a certificate decreasing from 57 percent in school year 2006-2007 to 42 percent in school year 2011-2012. Over the same time frame, the number of teachers holding associate's, bachelor's, or master's degrees increased from 43 percent to 55 percent. OIA has advised the RMI Ministry of Education that all uncertified teachers should be in a ministry-approved degree program to be individually eligible for salary support from sector grant, supplemental education grant, or Ebeye special needs funds, and that these teachers should be certified by school year 2015.[45]

---

[45]JEMFAC has not made a resolution requiring teacher certification or indicating that funds will be withheld; however, JEMFAC recommended at its March 2013 midyear meeting that a grant condition be placed on the fiscal year 2014 Ministry of Education budget stipulating that any uncertified teacher not enrolled in a ministry-approved training program would be ineligible for any compact-funded salary support.

We determined that data for 3 of the indicators could not be used to assess education sector progress for the compact as a whole because of data reliability problems.[46] For example, we found that the RMI changed the data source for some of the indicators it reported on during fiscal years 2007 through 2011. In fiscal years 2007 through 2010, the RMI reported Pacific Island Literacy Test data on student achievement for 4th graders, whereas in fiscal year 2011 it reported the Marshall Islands Standardized Test for 3rd, 6th and 8th graders, so year-to-year progress cannot be assessed because different grades and different tests were used.

Site-Visit Observations Relating to Progress in the RMI Education Sector

In January 2013, we made site visits to 6 of 12 public educational facilities in Majuro Atoll and 3 of 6 public educational facilities in Kwajalein Atoll, selected on the basis of available time and travel constraints.[47] The new and renovated classrooms that we visited all had desks, chairs, and chalkboards. Most of the fans and lighting that we observed were in working order at the time of our visit, as were the new bathrooms. However, many of the safety doors that we observed at our selected schools were either off their hinges and moved to one side or propped open with an object. Officials told us that this problem occurred because the doors had not been properly installed.[48]

When we visited the RMI in 2006, we were shown classrooms in the Marshall Islands High School that had collapsed ceilings. We found no such problems during our visit to this school in 2013. However, we did find that several of the water tanks at the school were not connected to

---

[46]We contacted the RMI government and requested additional information about activities it took to ensure the data for education indicators were reliable. The responses we received did not provide sufficient information for us to determine that the data were reliable.

[47]The site visits we made in the RMI were intended to illustrate educational conditions under the compact at school sites we visited. Our observations are not generalizable to all school sites throughout the RMI.

[48]Commenting on a draft of this report, the RMI stated that the door at one of the elementary schools where we observed this problem had been repaired and that repairs were under way at three other elementary schools. We have not verified this information. (See app. XI for a copy of the RMI's comments.)

any of the buildings.[49] At another school that we visited, Laura Elementary, classrooms in the new building had desks, chairs, and electricity, but an old building that was still used lacked electricity.[50] At Delap Elementary, the classrooms also had electricity. On Ebeye, we visited a school in Gugeegue that had consistent electricity, we were told. We observed chairs, desks, and textbooks on our visit. However, we were also shown one of the school buildings being used for classrooms though it was considered unsafe by the RMI's Project Management Unit.[51] (For information on compact-funded infrastructure projects in the education and health sectors, see app. II.)

Assessment of RMI Progress in Health

RMI Has Tracked Annual Indicators in Health since 2007, but We Found Problems with Data Reliability

The RMI established 26 indicators to measure progress toward its goal of improving primary health care in the RMI in 2006, and tracked them since 2007 (see app. VI for a list of the RMI's health indicators), according to the RMI's Ministry of Health.[52] We found that 1 of the subset of 5 indicators that we reviewed—tuberculosis prevalence rates—was sufficiently reliable to assess progress in the health sector for fiscal years 2009 through 2011 (see table 4).[53] While the number of tuberculosis

---

[49]Commenting on a draft of this report, the RMI stated that Ministry of Education maintenance crews were currently fixing the catchment tanks, which the crews had intentionally disconnected for repair purposes. We have not verified this information. (See app. XI for a copy of the RMI's comments.)

[50]Commenting on a draft of this report, the RMI indicated that all classrooms at Laura Elementary School are hooked up to power and that Ministry of Education Maintenance does not recall any complaints about the lack of power but some internal electrical problem might have occurred during our visit. We have not verified this information. (See app. XI for a copy of the RMI's comments.)

[51]Commenting on a draft of this report, the RMI noted that the old building mentioned has been abandoned and that a new three-classroom building has been constructed at Kwajalein Atoll High School. We have not verified this information. (See app. XI for a copy of the RMI's comments.)

[52]The RMI's indicators are identical to the Millennium Development Goals health-related indicators and use the same definitions. The Millennium Development Goals health-related indicators are found under three separate categories: improving maternal health, reducing child mortality, and combating HIV/AIDS, malaria, and other diseases.

[53]In 2009, the RMI began using the Center for Disease Control's EpiAnywhere web-based system to track tuberculosis cases and thus we decided not to include data from 2007 and 2008 in our data reliability assessment.

cases was 23 in fiscal year 2009, the number increased to 30 cases in fiscal year 2010 and then fell slightly to 29 in fiscal year 2011.[54]

Table 4: Subset of 5 of the 26 Republic of the Marshall Islands (RMI) Health Indicators Reviewed, with Observations on the Reliability of the Data to Measure Progress for the Compact as a Whole from 2007 through 2011

Indicator	Observations on data	Sufficiently reliable to measure progress over time? Yes, No, or No basis to judge
Immunization coverage (2-year-olds)	Proper data collection, timeliness, and accuracy of data prior to 2013 were problematic; low coverage rates for outer island data; and internal RMI disagreement regarding data.	No
Child mortality rate	For outer islands, there are ongoing problems with consistently collecting and reporting data; timeliness issues exist with reporting from Ebeye.	No
Diabetes rate	RMI lacked an explanation as to why rates are increasing other than increased screening; revisions to data with no explanation.	No basis to judge
Eliminate leprosy	RMI lacked an explanation as to why rates are increasing other than increased screening.	No basis to judge
Tuberculosis rate		Yes

Source: GAO analysis of RMI data.

Notes: Tuberculosis data for 2007 and 2008 are not included in the data we considered. By "sufficiently reliable," we mean that the likelihood of significant errors or incompleteness is minimal, and the use of the data would not lead to an incorrect or unintentional message. The indicator titles are shortened in the table; for the full indicator titles, see app. VI.

However, we determined that 2 of the subset of 5 health indicators that we reviewed were not sufficiently reliable because of various issues with data collection and reporting. For example, we determined that data reported for immunization coverage for 2-year-olds and the child mortality rate were not reliable due to the timeliness and accuracy of reporting and low coverage rates for data from the outer islands, all problems noted in the Ministry of Health's responses to our questions on data reliability. We found that for 2 other health indicators we had no basis to judge their reliability.

Site-Visit Observations Relating to Progress in the RMI Health Sector

During January 2013, we visited both hospitals in the RMI, one located on Majuro and the other on Ebeye island in the Kwajalein Atoll. We did not attempt to visit any health clinics in other atolls due to logistic considerations. During our 2006 visit to the Ebeye island hospital, we

---

[54]The RMI did not provide an explanation for the increases other than that it had improved its detection and monitoring for the disease.

GAO-13-675 Compacts of Free Association

were told that persistent problems with Ebeye's power supply continued to interrupt hospital services. In 2013, however, we were told that the Ebeye island hospital had regular electricity, which we observed at the time of our visit. This facility also appeared to be clean, and the selected medical and laboratory equipment that we examined was functioning. On our visit to the hospital in Majuro, we asked whether the dispensary maintained a drug formulary—a list of the required drugs on hand.[55] The hospital in Majuro provided us with a copy of its formulary, which was from 2007. The drugs and medical supplies that we spot-checked at the hospital were within their labeled expiration dates. (For information on compact-funded infrastructure projects in the education and health sectors, see app. II.)

FSM, RMI, and Bilateral Oversight Committees Are Aware of Data Reliability Problems in Compact Indicator Reports and of the Effect on Their Ability to Evaluate Progress

FSM and JEMCO

Education. In the annual education indicators report that it submitted to JEMCO from 2007 through 2011,[56] the FSM identified problems with the overall quality, and consistency, of the education data, as well as problems with timeliness in reporting. Additionally, the reports noted the need for training of the data managers and difficulties with the data systems.[57] In March 2012, JEMCO reaffirmed the need for reliable

---

[55]The RMI does not have an indicator that tracks the availability of essential drugs on hand in hospitals and dispensaries. Nonetheless, we visited the hospital pharmacy in Majuro and asked to look at the list of essential drugs; we discussed their availability and then checked to see whether their labeled expiration dates had passed.

[56]The annual reports are to be submitted by July 31 each year. The number of postsecondary scholarship recipients was added as an indicator in 2011, bringing the total number of education indicators to 21.

[57]The FSM Department of Education reported that staff in the state departments of education have been trained to enter data on education indicators into their management systems, and that state and National Government officials perform some checks of the data entered.

education data to evaluate performance in a resolution that required independent verification of performance indicators and data for the education sector, which the FSM was to communicate in a report due to OIA by July 1, 2013, prior to the August 2013 annual meeting.[58] In April 2013, the FSM Department of Education (National Government) addressed the JEMCO resolution by seeking proposals to conduct an independent verification of its performance indicators and data quality. The request for proposals stated that the project period was approximately 2 months, ending July 30, 2013, but it did not state whether a report on the results of the project would be prepared within that time frame.[59]

Health. The FSM reported on its 14 annual health indicators, comprehensively by state and for the National Government, in a July 2012 report by the FSM national Department of Health and Social Affairs covering fiscal years 2004 through 2011. The report noted limitations with some of the data, for example, that not all infant deaths in the outer islands were included in the infant mortality data.[60] In response to the report, JEMCO identified concerns regarding the reliability of data reported for the health indicators. For example, JEMCO noted concerns about the accuracy of the reported infant mortality rates as well as the reported number of encounters for primary health care services offered in community and dispensary settings, which the FSM tracked as a proxy measure of improved community-based primary health care. In its 2012 resolution JEMCO reaffirmed the need for reliable and quantifiable health data to evaluate performance and also required independent verification of performance indicators and data for the health sector; it required the

---

[58]JEMCO resolution 2012-MT-3.

[59]The project period stipulated in the request for proposals was May 24, 2013, to July 30, 2013.

[60]Previously, the OIA Health Fiscal Program Specialist had raised data quality concerns. A 2007 Compact Health Sector Performance Scorecard produced by the Health Fiscal Program Specialist noted that in order to measure performance accurately, the FSM's Department of Health and Social Affairs would need to standardize data collection and tabulation methods employed by each state, establish accepted timing intervals for collection and reporting, and ensure that outer island information is included. According to Department of Health and Social Affairs officials, health indicators are collected both through web-based data management systems and through compiling data collected manually. Officials also reported some checks on particular indicators, such as system checks to catch data entry errors and supervisory review of some indicators.

FSM to submit a report on the health indicators by July 1, 2013.[61] We inquired about the status of the FSM's effort to address the JEMCO resolution to conduct an independent verification of the health data, and the Department of Health and Social Affairs informed us that the FSM asked for an extension of the July deadline. According to OIA, the FSM did not budget sufficient funds for the assessment, and that is why the FSM needed an extension.

RMI and JEMFAC

Education. From fiscal years 2007 through 2011, the RMI reported data on its annual indicators in its Ministry of Education annual portfolio budget statements (hereafter, portfolios). The RMI Ministry of Education reported that data on educational indicators are entered quarterly into its data management system, and that schools generally provide their data before the established deadlines. The RMI also provided us with copies of the standard forms that it uses to collect data on educational indicators. The RMI's portfolios containing the indicator data did not explicitly identify limitations associated with the overall data; however, the portfolios included some notes describing limitations for a couple of indicators. For example, one note indicated that student teacher ratios did not include private schools. JEMFAC has not sought an independent review of RMI education indicator data quality.

Health. The RMI Ministry of Health issued an annual health data report for each year from 2007 through 2011.[62] The RMI also noted in its 2011 annual health data report that immunization coverage data showed a significant drop because of data entry problems, mainly in terms of lateness in entering data and an inability to keep track of children moving from one locality to another. The RMI Ministry of Health reported it uses a number of different international databases to track its health indicator progress such as WebIZ for immunizations and EpiAnywhere for tuberculosis. The Ministry of Health reported that they have undertaken a couple of different data assessments to improve data accuracy, as well as made efforts to improve reporting from Ebeye and the outer islands. Among the checks the Ministry of Health reported that it conducts to ensure the accuracy of the tuberculosis rate indicator is comparing the

---

[61]JEMCO Resolution 2012-MT-3.

[62]The annual health data report for 2007 was combined with the report for 2008 and issued as a single report.

data entered into the database with results from lab tests, X-rays, and clinical visits.

In 2009, JEMFAC noted that the RMI health data were unreliable because of discrepancies related to outer island data and infant mortality rates. Other outside reports also questioned how the Ministry of Health handled other data on disease incidence, prevalence, and mortality.[63] In 2010, JEMFAC required that the Ministry of Health initiate and complete an assessment of the reliability of all its health data-management practices by September 30, 2011. The ministry obtained technical assistance from a United Nations Volunteer to address the requirement. However, the volunteer technical expert only stayed 10 months, leaving in July 2012, and the position was still vacant as of July 2013, according to the Ministry of Health. The RMI had not provided JEMFAC with the required report as of June 2013.[64]

---

[63]The OIA's former Health Fiscal Program Specialist, who retired in December 2012, told us that the RMI's Ministry of Health has no consistent framework for collecting the data, that record keeping is poor, and that data entry is inconsistent.

[64]Entities such as the RMI Economic Policy, Planning, and Statistics Office (EPPSO), the Secretariat of the Pacific Community (SPC), and the World Health Organization have also raised concerns about the quality of the health data reported by the RMI Ministry of Health. Both EPSSO and SPC, noting the underreporting of infant deaths in the RMI's outer islands, estimated that half of all infant deaths in the RMI were not reported at all, which created uncertainty as to the most common causes of infant deaths. SPC and the World Health Organization noted that the RMI's health statistics are outdated by 2 to 3 years and sometimes by as much as 7 years. EPPSO found that outer island immunization coverage rates for children under the age of 2 were at least 30 percent lower in select outer island groups than official health reports indicated. A United Nations Millennium Development Goal specialist also discovered data problems. He reviewed data from the ministry's maternal and child health program and found that his recalculated immunization coverage rates ranged from 48 to 67 percent for Majuro, while the rates computed by the ministry ranged from 80 to 90 percent.

FSM and RMI Face Financial Accountability Challenges; Oversight Bodies Are Hindered by Limitations

The single audit reports[65] we reviewed indicated challenges to ensuring accountability of compact and noncompact U.S. funds in the FSM and RMI. For example, these governments' single audits showed repeat findings and persistent problems in noncompliance with U.S. program requirements, such as accounting for equipment. The United States has taken steps regarding the accountability of compact funds, such as establishing the Chuuk Financial Control Commission, but Interior has not coordinated with other U.S. agencies regarding the risk status of the FSM and the RMI for noncompact funds. Furthermore, the offices responsible for compact administration in the FSM, RMI, and United States faced limitations hindering their ability to conduct compact oversight. For example, OIA experienced a staffing shortage that disproportionately affected compact grant oversight compared to other OIA activities, with 5 of 11 planned positions filled in 2012.

---

[65]The Single Audit Act adopted the single audit concept to help meet the needs of federal agencies for grantee oversight, as well as grantees' needs for single, uniformly structured audits. Rather than being a detailed review of individual grants or programs, the single audit is an organization-wide financial statement audit that includes the audit of the Schedule of Expenditures of Federal Awards and also focuses on internal control and the recipient's compliance with laws and regulations governing the federal financial assistance received. The act also required grantees to address material noncompliance and internal control weaknesses in a corrective action plan, which is to be submitted to appropriate federal officials. The act further required that single audits be performed in accordance with generally accepted government auditing standards issued by GAO. These standards provide a framework for conducting high-quality financial audits with competence, integrity, objectivity, and independence.

Financial Accountability in the FSM Was Mixed

Single Audits Showed FSM National Government Faced Challenges, While Chuuk and Pohnpei Demonstrated Financial Accountability Improvement

In fiscal years 2006 through 2011,[66] the FSM National Government single audit reports indicated that the government faced financial accountability challenges. However, the single audit reports for Chuuk and Pohnpei state governments demonstrated improvement in financial accountability: financial statement audit opinions improved and the number of material weaknesses[67] and significant deficiencies [68] declined. As an example of the remaining challenges for the FSM National Government, its 2011 single audit report identified problems with the extent of noncompliance with program requirements, such as preparing required quarterly reports. These reports are important because OIA uses them for oversight of the amended compact. Furthermore, the National Government's 2011 single audit report contained several repeat findings—problems noted in previous audits that had not been corrected for several years. For a detailed summary of our review of the FSM single audit reports, see appendix VII.

The following briefly summarizes our analysis of the single audits for the FSM National Government and the state governments of Chuuk and Pohnpei.

- *Financial reporting:* FSM National Government single audit reports conveyed that the government was not able to account fully for its use

---

[66]The scope for this report is generally fiscal years 2007 through 2011; however, we are including fiscal year 2006 because the last single audit report discussed in our prior report (GAO-07-163) was for fiscal year 2005.

[67]American Institute of Certified Public Accountants, Statement on Auditing Standard No. 115, "Communicating Internal Control Related Matters Identified in an Audit," states that a material weakness is a deficiency, or a combination of deficiencies, in internal control indicating a reasonable possibility that a material misstatement of the entity's financial statements will not be prevented, or detected and corrected, on a timely basis. A deficiency in internal control exists when the design or operation of a control does not allow management or employees, in the normal course of performing their assigned functions, to prevent, or detect and correct, misstatements on a timely basis.

[68]American Institute of Certified Public Accountants, Statement on Auditing Standard No. 115, "Communicating Internal Control Related Matters Identified in an Audit," states that a significant deficiency is a deficiency or a combination of deficiencies in internal control that is less severe than a material weakness, yet important enough to merit attention by those charged with governance.

of compact or noncompact funds for fiscal years 2006 through 2008. Chuuk's single audit reports continued to identify financial accountability weaknesses, primarily because Chuuk's financial statements did not contain information on its land leases in fiscal years 2009 through 2011. For fiscal years 2006 through 2011, Pohnpei received an unqualified opinion[69] on its financial statements included in its single audit reports. (For additional details, see app. VII.)

- *Compliance with requirements of major federal programs:*[70] The FSM National Government continued to be noncompliant with the terms and conditions of major federal programs in fiscal year 2011 in each of its three major programs. Furthermore, its fiscal year 2011 single audit report included four material weaknesses and eight significant deficiencies. The FSM National Government continued to have findings that have not been corrected for several years. For example, seven findings had recurred at least three times in the 4 years prior to 2011.[71] In addition, the FSM National Government had consistently lacked the ability to prevent disbursing funds in excess of available funds in each year for the previous 2 years and lacked the ability to accurately report financial information in each of the previous 4 years. We believe recurring weaknesses in internal controls increase the risk that assets are susceptible to misuse. In contrast, Chuuk's fiscal year 2011 single audit report demonstrated improvement in compliance with major federal programs. Whereas Chuuk previously had been considered noncompliant in fiscal years 2006 through 2010, it was considered materially compliant in fiscal year 2011. Pohnpei's single

---

[69]An unqualified opinion is given when the auditor is reasonably assured that the financial statements are free of material misstatements.

[70]OMB Circular A-133 states "the auditor shall determine whether the auditee has complied with laws, regulations, and the provisions of contracts or grant agreements that may have direct and material effect on each of its major programs. The auditor uses a risk-based approach to determine which program is a major program. This risk-based approach includes consideration of current and prior audit experience, oversight by federal agencies, and pass-through entities, and inherent risk of the federal program."

[71]GAO, *Standards for Internal Control in the Federal Government,* GAO/AIMD-00-21.3.1, (Washington, D.C.: November 1999), pp. 20-21: "Managers are to (1) promptly evaluate findings from audits and other reviews, including those showing deficiencies and recommendations reported by auditors and others who evaluate agencies' operations, (2) determine proper actions in response to findings and recommendations from audits and reviews, and (3) complete, within established time frames, all actions that correct or otherwise resolve the matters brought to management's attention."

audit reports also demonstrated improvement, as the state government was noncompliant with the requirements of federal programs in fiscal years 2006 and 2007 but was considered materially compliant in fiscal years 2008 through 2011. See appendix VII for additional information.

- *Timeliness:* The FSM National Government and Chuuk did not submit their 2006 single audit reports on time due to a delay in the reconciliation of accounting records.[72] In fiscal years 2007 through 2011, however, the FSM National Government and Chuck submitted their single audit reports on time. Pohnpei met the deadline for submitting single audit reports during the entire period, fiscal years 2006 through 2011. (For additional details, see appendix VII.)

FSM Audit Offices Conducted Program Audits and Found Instances of Weak Internal Controls That Could Increase Risk of Waste, Fraud, and Abuse

The FSM has a national audit office, the Office of the National Public Auditor (ONPA), and Pohnpei has a Public Auditor. According to ONPA officials, ONPA has a staff of 15 in Pohnpei and 5 in Chuuk.[73] According to state officials, the Pohnpei state government's Office of the Public Auditor (OPA) has a professional staff of 8.[74] Both the ONPA and OPA identified internal control weaknesses in their audits of the FSM National Government and state government that could lead to waste, fraud, and abuse. The following are examples from reports issued by the ONPA.

- An audit report on the National Government's payroll operating controls for fiscal years 2010 through 2012 found overpayments to

---

[72]The FSM National Government's single audit cannot be completed until the states' single audits are completed. Thus, if any state is late, the FSM National Government's audit will also be late. Chuuk submitted its 2006 single audit late.

[73]According to ONPA officials, the ONPA was established to conduct audits and investigations to recommend improvements in government operations, efficiency, and accountability for the public's benefit. The office conducts financial and compliance, economy and efficiency, and program audits.

[74]The 2005 Constitution of the State of Chuuk, Article VII—Finance, Section 9, requires the appointment of a Public Auditor by the Governor and approval by the Senate. According to ONPA officials, a Chuuk Public Auditor has never been appointed but Chuuk state will establish an independent, fully operational public auditor's office in fiscal year 2014, and funds have been sought under the compact to support the office.

employees including payments to active and terminated employees and for hours worked but not authorized.[75]

- A report on the Chuuk State Department of Health Services found that the department did not implement a procurement and inventory control system ensuring the efficient use of funds and the timely distribution of medications to recipients. This program was funded by the amended compact health sector grant.[76]

- A report on the Chuuk Department of Education found that it failed to provide many students with textbooks, to hold schools and students accountable for lost books, and to ensure that classroom lessons followed the approved state curriculum. This program was funded by amended compact education sector grant.[77]

In fiscal years 2008 through 2011, the Pohnpei state government's OPA also conducted audits that identified findings related to internal control weaknesses potentially leading to waste, fraud, and abuse.[78] For example, its September 2008 audit report found weak internal controls in the issuance of pharmaceutical and medical supplies from the Pohnpei

---

[75]Office of the National Public Auditor, *Audit of FSM Payroll Operating Controls, Fiscal Years 2010, 2011, 2012 through May*, Report No. 2012-04 (Palikir, Pohnpei: Aug. 9, 2012). Although the report's issuance date was outside our scope (fiscal years 2006 to 2011), the ONPA audit covered fiscal years 2010 and 2011 which are included in our scope. This report included 7 findings and 20 recommendations. Management provided corrective action plans to resolve these findings. As of June 2013, the ONPA had not performed a follow-up audit to ensure that appropriate corrective actions were taken.

[76]Office of the National Public Auditor, *Audit of Chuuk State Department of Health Services' Procurement and Inventory Management System*, Report Number 2010-03 (Pal ker, Pohnpei: Feb. 10, 2010). This report included 8 findings and over 30 recommendations. Management generally agreed with the findings and provided corrective action plans. As of June 2013, the ONPA is performing a follow-up audit to ensure that appropriate corrective actions were taken.

[77]Office of the National Public Auditor, *Audit of Chuuk State Department of Education Textbooks and Instructional Material,* Report No. 2010-01 (Paliker, Pohnpei: Feb. 9, 2010). The report included 9 recommendations. Management did not respond to the findings and recommendations. As of June 2013, the ONPA is performing but has not completed a follow-up audit to ensure that appropriate corrective actions were taken.

[78]According to government officials, the Pohnpei state government's Office of the Public Auditor was established in 1984. Its mission is to evaluate state and local government operations to provide useful and objective information to executive, legislative, management and citizens.

Central Medical Supply Unit and other sections of the Department of Health Services.[79] The amended compact was the primary source of funding. The report noted the lack of assurance that recipients actually received all items indicated in the receipts because there was not a reliable audit trail for the issuance of pharmaceutical and medical supplies.

RMI Faced Financial Accountability Challenges

Single Audits in the RMI Revealed Increased Financial Accountability Challenges

RMI single audit reports for fiscal years 2006 through 2011 demonstrated an increase in material weaknesses in noncompliance with the requirements of federal programs. For example, the 2006 single audit report identified 4 material weaknesses in compliance with federal awards and about $5.7 million in unresolved questioned costs.[80] However, the 2011 single audit report identified 8 material weaknesses and about $7.4 million in unresolved questioned costs as of September 30, 2011.[81] While reports for fiscal years 2006 through 2010 were submitted on time, the 2011 single audit report was late. For a detailed summary of our review of the RMI single audit reports, see appendix VII.

---

[79]Office of the Public Auditor, Pohnpei State Government, *Department of Health Service Procurement, Audit Report,* No. 006-09 (Kolonia, Pohnpei: Aug. 5, 2010). Furthermore, the report observed that management did not review the turnover of pharmaceutical and medical supplies for the audit period and had not established a minimum level of stock that should be maintained. Consequently, the OPA made five recommendations to improve the accountability over inventory management at the Department of Health Services. An OPA audit official told us that their recommendations were implemented but, as of June 2013, they had not completed a follow-up audit.

[80]OMB Circular A-133 states that "Questioned costs are those costs questioned by an auditor for one of these three reasons: (1) They resulted from a violation or possible violation of a provision of a law, regulation, contract, grant, cooperative agreement, or other agreement or document governing the use of federal funds, including funds used to match federal funds; or (2) at the time of the audit, they are not supported by adequate documentation; or (3) the costs incurred appear unreasonable and do not reflect the actions a prudent person would take in the circumstances."

[81]At the March 2013 JEMFAC midyear meeting, the OIA recommended that the unexpended 2011 and 2012 funds not be allocated to the RMI until these questioned costs are resolved. Commenting on a draft of this report, RMI officials stated that the RMI Secretary of Finance took steps to better manage the audit fieldwork process and reduced the 2012 questioned costs to approximately $35,000 and also began a detailed examination of all prior year questioned costs. At its 2013 annual meeting in August 2013, JEMFAC did not allocate the unexpended 2011 and 2012 funds.

The following briefly summarizes our analysis of the RMI single audits.

- *Financial reporting:* In fiscal years 2006 through 2011,[82] the RMI received an unqualified audit opinion on each of its annual financial statements. (See app. VII for a list of the opinions on financial statements in the RMI's audit reports for fiscal years 2006 through 2011.)

- *Compliance with requirements of major federal programs:* [83] The RMI single audit reports indicated they were noncompliant with the requirements of federal programs in fiscal years 2006 through 2011. The fiscal year 2011 single audit report included eight findings that were considered material weaknesses. Some findings were related to compact grants and others to noncompact funding. Furthermore, several of the weaknesses were not corrected over several years. For example, seven of the eight material weaknesses reported in the fiscal year 2011 single audit recurred at least once in the 2 prior years and five had recurred in 3 out of the 4 previous years.[84] For example, each year for 4 years prior to fiscal year 2011, the RMI was not able to provide supporting documentation for its expenses and an adequate accounting for its fixed assets to meet the requirements in the fiscal procedures agreement. Furthermore, we believe that recurring weaknesses in internal controls increase the risk that assets are susceptible to misuse. Also, the fiscal year 2011 RMI single audit report demonstrated that the RMI did not comply with some of the requirements of federal programs. For example, the RMI disbursed $1 million in compact sector grants to the Marshall Islands National

---

[82]The scope for this report is generally fiscal years 2007 through 2011; however, we are including fiscal year 2006 because the last single audit report discussed in our prior report (GAO-07-163) was for fiscal year 2005.

[83]OMB Circular A-133 states, "The auditor shall determine whether the auditee has complied with laws, regulations, and the provisions of contracts or grant agreements that may have direct and material effect on each of its major programs. The auditor uses a risk-based approach to determine which program is a major program. This risk-based approach includes consideration of current and prior audit experience, oversight by federal agencies, and pass-through entities, and inherent risk of the federal program."

[84]GAO/AIMD-00-21.3.1, pp. 20-21: "Managers are to (1) promptly evaluate findings from audits and other reviews, including those showing deficiencies and recommendations reported by auditors and others who evaluate agencies' operations, (2) determine proper actions in response to findings and recommendations from audits and reviews, and (3) complete, within established time frames, all actions that correct or otherwise resolve the matters brought to management's attention."

Telecommunications Authority without an audit.[85] In addition, the auditors reported that documentation supporting expenditures from various ministries could not be located and resulted in questioned costs totaling approximately $1.1 million; other questioned costs were also identified for various reasons in the 2011 single audit. (For additional details, see app. VII.)

- *Timeliness:* For fiscal years 2006 through 2010, the RMI met the single audit report submission deadline. In July 2012, the RMI contacted OIA and requested an extension to file its 2011 single audit by September 30, 2012. OIA granted the extension, stating no adverse action would be taken if the single audit was completed and received by OIA by September 30, 2012. However, RMI submitted its fiscal year 2011 report in February 2013, 8 months late.[86] According to the RMI Ministry of Finance, the 2011 single audit report was late because of staff turnover, computer system issues, and late reconciliation of general ledger and bank accounts. As a result, the 2011 single audit was not received by the United States until 17 months after the end of the year in which the reported findings were identified; OIA took no adverse action. (For additional details, see app. VII.)

RMI Audit Office Identifies Fraud Indicators in Audit Reports

RMI Office of the Auditor General (OAG) officials also told us that previous annual single audits reported fraud indicators (e.g., numerous findings on noncompliance with procurement requirements) that were not looked into by the RMI government in office at that time.[87] The current OAG indicated that if the RMI government at that time, including the then OAG, had investigated the reported procurement issues, the recent fraud cases in the Ministry of Health and Human Services and Ministry of

---

[85]The grant award did not undergo a separate OMB Circular A-133 audit, as required.

[86]The Compliance Supplement included in OMB Circular A-133 no longer allowed federal agencies to consider requests for a time extension to file single audit reports for fiscal years 2009 through 2011.

[87]The OAG coordinates the RMI annual single audit and other component audits. Furthermore, for fiscal years 2006 through 2011, the OAG performed audits of several component units and performed a performance audit of the Majuro Atoll Waste Company. The OAG told us that it plans to perform additional performance audits in the future.

Finance might have been uncovered earlier.[88] (For additional details, see app. VII).

OIA Has Taken Some Steps to Improve FSM and RMI Financial Accountability

Compact Grants

Working through JEMCO and JEMFAC, OIA has led actions to improve financial accountability of compact funds and has recommended further actions.

- The improvement in Chuuk audit reports was the result of cooperation between the JEMCO and Chuuk state government. For example, Chuuk's fiscal year 2004 single audit report included 30 findings and unresolved questioned costs totaling approximately $6.7 million. In fiscal year 2005, the JEMCO established the Chuuk Financial Control Commission (CFCC) to assist the Chuuk government in managing its finances. Consequently, Chuuk's fiscal year 2011 single audit report identified 5 findings with no unresolved questioned costs. According to a CFCC official, the CFCC has played an important role in restoring and maintaining the integrity of compact sector grant expenditures.[89]

- The JEMFAC reported after its review of the RMI fiscal year 2011 single audit report that unresolved questioned costs had significantly increased over the previous 4 years. At the JEMFAC midyear meeting held on March14, 2013, discussion included the issue of the RMI's inability to comply with requirements regarding allowable costs, cash management, equipment, and real property management, among other issues, as well as the related unresolved questioned costs reported in the 2011 single audit, which totaled over $5 million. The RMI Secretary of Finance told OIA officials that the RMI had recently taken positive steps to resolve outstanding questioned costs and to

[88]According to RMI officials, from 2009 to 2011, there was ongoing fraud at the Ministries of Finance and Health. The RMI Attorney General's Office has been prosecuting the fraud, which resulted in several convictions. During this time, the RMI OAG has also assisted the RMI Attorney General's Office in its fraud investigation.

[89]See also Kevin O'Keefe, Deborah Milks, and Jeanne Yamamura, *Report of Observations and Preliminary Recommendations to the Working Group Specified by Resolution JEMCO-MT-2011-7, The Role of the Chuuk Financial Control Commission (CFCC)*, (Honolulu, Hawaii: Graduate School USA, August 2011).

strengthen the ministry's internal controls; nevertheless, OIA recommended that JEMFAC refrain from allocating unexpended grant funds from fiscal year 2011 and fiscal year 2012 until the RMI demonstrated that it had resolved all current questioned costs. At its annual meeting in August 2013, JEMFAC did not allocate the unexpended 2011 and 2012 funds.

Although OIA has authority to impose special conditions or restrictions for unsatisfactory performance or failure to comply with grant terms, OIA officials have preferred to work through the JEMCO and JEMFAC committees rather than take unilateral action. While no official "high risk" designation exists in the amended compacts or fiscal procedures agreements, the fiscal procedures agreements' provisions governing grants administration allow the same special conditions to be applied to amended compact grants that exist for other high-risk grantees receiving federal assistance. OIA officials told us that they treat the amended compact funds as high risk and provide special conditions through the JEMCO and JEMFAC resolutions, such as requiring the acquisition of technical or management assistance, requiring additional reporting and monitoring, or withholding funds.

Other U.S. Noncompact Grants

Regarding financial accountability of noncompact grants, OIA has not coordinated the federal response to audit findings that affect programs of more than one agency. Nor have OIA or other federal agencies designated the FSM or the RMI as high-risk grantees, which would allow those agencies to impose special conditions on their grants such as requiring additional reporting and monitoring.

- Single audit reports show compliance problems for compact and noncompact grants. For example, the 2011 FSM National Government single audit reported that for one special education grant, the FSM, unable to draw down funds from the grant account because the period of funds availability had closed, improperly reimbursed itself from a different grant account that was still open. The same single audit also reported that the FSM National Government submitted financial reports for Transportation's Airport Improvement Project grant that did not agree with underlying financial records. According to OIA officials, Interior has not coordinated the response of federal agencies to these audit findings because of its focus on its responsibility for oversight of the amended compact funding.

- According to Interior officials, while Interior and other U.S. agencies may designate the FSM and the RMI as high-risk grantees for noncompact grants if the grantee has a history of performance problems, as of June 2013, no agencies have done so, potentially because of the lack of coordination between OIA and other grantors. Education officials noted that the department looks to see if there are systemic problems when designating a grant recipient as high risk but they have not formally assessed this status for the FSM or RMI. HHS officials believe the department's noncompact funds are at risk, but HHS has not conducted a systematic review of FSM and RMI audit results or considered whether the grantees should be considered high risk. OIA officials told us they have not undertaken a formal analysis to determine whether Interior noncompact funds should have a high-risk designation and have not held formal discussions with other grantor agencies (e.g., with Education, Transportation, or other grantors) regarding this issue.

Staffing Constraints Hindered Oversight Offices in Fulfilling Their Oversight Responsibilities

FSM Compact Management Unit's Oversight Limited by Staffing Constraints and Lack of Authority

FSM officials stated in January 2013 that staff constraints in the Office of Statistics, Budget and Economic Management, Overseas Development Assistance, and Compact Management's (SBOC) Division of Compact Management limit the division's ability to conduct oversight.[90] The Division of Compact Management is responsible for, among other things, day-to-day communications with JEMCO and the U.S. government and oversight of compact implementation, including coordination with recipients of compact grants to ensure effective and efficient use of compact funds. FSM officials told us that the division is currently staffed by three staff members who provide compact oversight for the FSM National Government and the four states across six sectors. However, FSM officials told us that they need additional staff so they can conduct more oversight activities.

---

[90]Prior to 2008, the FSM's predecessor office to SBOC, the Office of Compact Management, served as the FSM's primary compact oversight office. In 2006, we reported that the Office of Compact Management lacked sufficient staff to oversee compact-funded programs. At that time, the Office of Compact Management had five staff members, including its director; additional staff from finance and economic affairs departments were detailed to the office to assist with compact-related responsibilities. See GAO-07-163.

In addition to the staffing shortage, FSM officials told us that the Division of Compact Management is hampered by its lack of authority to ensure that the National Government and the four states comply with compact requirements. For example, while the National Government and any subgrantees, including the four states, are required by the compact's fiscal procedures agreements to provide quarterly reports with data and information on progress toward sector performance indicators, the Division of Compact Management does not have the authority to enforce this requirement if the National Government and states do not comply. In this case, FSM officials will sometimes request that the Department of Finance withhold quarterly allotments of compact funds until an entity submits the required information or, if necessary, identify issues for OIA to address.

RMI Compact Management Unit's Oversight Limited by Staff Constraints and Lack of Authority

According to RMI officials, staff constraints in the Office of Compact Implementation (OCI) limit the office's ability to conduct oversight and enforce compact requirements across multiple sectors and operations in numerous atolls. OCI has responsibility for all issues related to the compact and is also responsible for preparation and follow-up for all JEMFAC meetings, responses to GAO reports, and preparations for any congressional hearings on compact-related matters. RMI officials told us that the office is currently staffed by two people—a director and a foreign service officer—who run the office with three divisions.[91] RMI officials also stated they depended on officials from other government agencies to help them fulfill their responsibilities. For example, OCI uses the legal advisor of the Ministry of Foreign Affairs to assist with compact issues since the OCI's Division of Compact Legal Affairs has not filled its legal position.

Additionally, OCI officials told us they are hampered by their lack of authority to require that the RMI ministries implementing projects funded by sector grants comply with compact requirements. For example, OCI works through the Ministry of Foreign Affairs or the Office of the Chief Secretary when other RMI ministries or offices have not submitted compact-related reports. RMI officials said the government has not resolved the question of who within the RMI government has the authority to withhold funds to ensure compliance. According to RMI comments on

---

[91]The three divisions are the Division of Performance Based Budgeting, the Division of Economic and Budget Strategy, and the Division of Compact Legal Affairs. Prior to the establishment of OCI within the Ministry of Foreign Affairs in 2008, the RMI Chief Secretary was responsble for compact implementation and oversight.

our draft report, the Office of the Chief Secretary does not have authority to withhold funds from ministries or offices to compel them to comply with compact requirements (see app. XI).

OIA's Compact Oversight Limited by Staff Constraints

From fiscal years 2011 through 2013, OIA experienced staff constraints, particularly in the Honolulu field office and in the FSM, that limited its ability to carry out its compact oversight responsibilities. In 2010, OIA created a plan that provided detailed staffing projections across OIA for fiscal years 2010 through 2014. To ensure effective oversight for the amended compacts, OIA projected a need for 8 staff in the Honolulu field office, 2 field staff in the FSM, and 1 field staff in the RMI for fiscal years 2011 through 2013, a total of 11 staff.[92] (See app. VIII for the plan's detailed staffing projections.) However, in 2011 and 2012, OIA had a total of 5 staff for compact oversight: 4 staff in its Honolulu field office and 1 field staff in the RMI. In March 2013, OIA filled 1 of the 2 projected FSM field staff positions.

The OIA 2010 workforce plan projected the need for 50 staff for all of its divisions in fiscal years 2010 through 2014; it projected that existing resources would allow OIA to fund a total of 43 staff during this period. However, actual staffing levels were less than 43 in 2011 and 2012. Though compact oversight staff would represent 22 percent of total projected staff in the plan, compact oversight staff represented 12 percent and 14 percent, respectively, of actual OIA total staff in fiscal years 2011 and 2012. As a result, OIA's staffing shortage disproportionately affected compact grant oversight compared to other OIA activities. See table 5.

[92]For Honolulu, the plan's eight staff positions included one lead program grants specialist, two education grants specialists, one health grants specialist, and four fiscal program specialists. In the plan, OIA stressed the need for more fiscal program specialists in order to strengthen oversight. According to OIA's workforce plan, fiscal program specialists provide grants oversight and monitoring of projects. For example, the fiscal program specialist staffed to the Honolulu field office provides oversight for the environment, private sector development, and public sector capacity building sectors.

Table 5: Office of Insular Affairs (OIA) Staffing, Fiscal Years 2010 through 2014

	Projected need (2010-2014)	Actual staff	
		2011	2012
Total OIA staff	50	41	37
Compact oversight staff[a]	11 (22%)	5 (12%)	5 (14%)
Other staff	39 (78%)	36 (88%)	32 (87%)

Source: GAO analysis based on OIA' data.

Notes: Percentages may not add up to 100 due to rounding. Data are from OIA's 2010 workforce plan and OIA's 2013 and 2014 budget justification documents.

[a]These figures include staff in Honolulu, the FSM, and the RMI directly responsible for compact oversight. Additional OIA staff support compact oversight from Washington, D.C.

According to OIA officials, the following three factors contributed to the staffing shortages affecting compact oversight in fiscal years 2011 and 2012.

- *Budget constraints and uncertainties:* OIA officials said budget constraints and uncertainties prevented the office from hiring staff and filling vacant positions as outlined in the workforce plan. OIA noted that the plan assumed sufficient budgetary resources, and with enacted budgets in fiscal years 2010 through 2013, OIA could not hire additional staff. OIA officials also cited budget uncertainties for fiscal years 2012 and 2013 as a factor that kept them from filling the second education grants specialist position.

- *OIA priorities:* OIA management did not fill compact-related vacancies because of other priorities, such as filling headquarters-based positions before filling field positions. For example, an OIA official said that OIA management held back some available funding in hopes of staffing a Guam field office.

- *Lack of qualified candidates:* OIA officials also noted that in 2011 OIA posted the vacancy for the second education grants specialist position in Honolulu but did not receive sufficiently qualified candidates, which prevented the office from hiring.

Staffing shortages, particularly those in the Honolulu field office, have negatively affected OIA's compact oversight in the FSM and the RMI. While oversight activities, site visits, and required meetings occurred, OIA noted the following oversight gaps:

- In a 2010 report, Interior's Office of the Inspector General reported that OIA's compact oversight was hindered by the lack of an FSM field representative to support oversight efforts, despite the fact that the FSM received about $100 million in grant funds, more than any other insular area.[93] Additionally, the report questioned whether OIA was effectively utilizing existing staff in the Honolulu field office.

- One OIA official said that the Honolulu field office's staffing shortage hinder OIA's ability to scrutinize financial reports and provide feedback to both countries. This official also stated that without a second person working on education sector compact assistance, OIA cannot thoroughly analyze education budgets, which results in high-level recommendations to the JEMCO and JEMFAC rather than specific recommendations that address issues such as the potential misuse of funds. Noting that the RMI experienced an increase in unquestioned costs over a period of 3 years, the OIA official stated that if the Honolulu office had a second education grants specialist, OIA could identify these issues earlier and support the OIA audit liaison in following up on issues identified in the single audits.

Conclusions

At the midpoint of the 20-year amended compact assistance term, the FSM and RMI face critical challenges in compact implementation. During the first 10 years, the FSM and the RMI spent most of their funds for education and health, sectors prioritized in the compact agreements. However, because of data reliability issues, neither country can demonstrate whether it has made progress toward its goals in these sectors. Now, with 10 years of amended compact sector funding left, both countries must quickly plan for reduced grant resources and resolve the accountability issues that have plagued them to date so that they can fully utilize the funds and time left to achieve their goals.

Both countries must complete plans that address annual decrements in compact funding and determine new revenue sources that will replace compact grant assistance in 2023. Despite multiple JEMCO and JEMFAC resolutions calling for the countries to produce these plans, the FSM National Government has yet to develop a plan that shows how it will address budgetary and economic challenges through 2023 and support the states in adjusting to the annual decrements, while the RMI

---

[93]In March 2013, OIA hired one of two projected FSM field representatives.

government has yet to develop a plan that demonstrates how it will adjust to the annual decrements. In the absence of these plans, JEMCO and JEMFAC will face challenges ensuring that annual grant assistance for both countries is allocated in a sustainable manner.

Ongoing problems with data reliability exist for both countries. Without reliable data, the countries cannot assess progress toward their goals in the education and health sectors and cannot effectively use results data for setting priorities and allocating resources aimed at improving performance. The lack of reliable data also hampers the ability of JEMCO and JEMFAC to oversee compact expenditures and assess the countries' progress toward all its goals in the education and health sectors.

The FSM's and RMI's single audits continue to identify long-standing and recurring findings, which if addressed could allow both countries to more effectively use U.S. resources and diminish potential losses that arise from fraud, waste, and abuse. Given these recurring audit findings, both compact and noncompact U.S. funds are at risk. Interventions by JEMCO were effective in Chuuk in bringing improved financial accountability; however, similar JEMCO and JEMFAC interventions have not been undertaken for the FSM National Government or the RMI. Furthermore, U.S. grants provided separately from the amended compact by multiple agencies are at risk. Although OIA has a lead role regarding audit matters, it has not formally coordinated with other U.S. agencies to address audit findings, nor has it assessed whether its own noncompact grants should be classified as high risk. Moreover, other federal agencies whose grants may be at risk have not routinely considered designating either country as a high-risk grantee. Such consideration could enable U.S. agencies to enforce conditions and restrictions on noncompact grant funds they provide, thus improving the oversight and management of the funds.

Finally, although the majority of grants administered by OIA are amended compact grants, OIA's amended compact oversight function was disproportionally affected by staffing shortages. While budget constraints prevented OIA from hiring the total number of staff it needed to conduct oversight for all of its grants, decisions to staff other OIA divisions rather than hire compact oversight staff affected OIA's ability to ensure compact funds were efficiently and effectively used.

Recommendations for Executive Action

We recommend that the Secretary of the Interior take the following five actions:

In order to improve the ability of the U.S. agencies participating in the JEMCO and JEMFAC committees to conduct required oversight of compact funds,

- direct the Director of Insular Affairs, as Chairman of JEMCO, to coordinate with other JEMCO-member U.S. agencies to have JEMCO take all necessary steps, or, as the administrator of compact grants, to directly take all necessary steps, to ensure that the FSM (1) completes satisfactory plans to address annual decrements in compact funds, (2) produces reliable indicator data used to track progress in education and health, and (3) addresses all single audit findings in a timely manner;[94] and

- direct the Director of Insular Affairs, as Chairman of the JEMFAC, to coordinate with other JEMFAC-member U.S. agencies to have JEMFAC take all necessary steps, or, as the administrator of compact grants, to directly take all necessary steps, to ensure that the RMI (1) completes satisfactory plans to address annual decrements in compact funds, (2) produces reliable indicator data used to track progress in education and health, and (3) addresses all single audit findings in a timely manner.

In order to improve financial accountability of noncompact U.S. grant assistance provided to the FSM and the RMI,

- consult with other grantor agencies to determine whether the FSM National Government or any FSM states meet the criteria to be designated as a high-risk grant recipient for noncompact funds, or whether other steps should be taken to improve accountability; and

- consult with other grantor agencies to determine whether the RMI meets the criteria to be designated as a high-risk grant recipient for

---

[94]GAO/AIMD-00-21.3.1, pp. 20-21: "Managers are to (1) promptly evaluate findings from audits and other reviews, including those showing deficiencies and recommendations reported by auditors and others who evaluate agencies' operations, (2) determine proper actions in response to findings and recommendations from audits and reviews, and (3) complete, within established time frames, all actions that correct or otherwise resolve the matters brought to management's attention."

noncompact funds, or whether other steps should be taken to improve accountability.

In order to ensure that Interior is providing appropriate resources for oversight and monitoring of the FSM and RMI compacts,

- take actions to correct the disproportionate staffing shortage related to compact grant implementation and oversight.

Agency Comments and Our Evaluation

We provided a draft of this report for comment to Interior, Education, HHS, and State and also to the FSM National Government and the government of the RMI. Interior, the FSM National Government, and the government of the RMI provided formal written comments on the draft report, which are reprinted in appendixes IX, X, and XI, respectively, and which we summarize below. Education and HHS had no comments on the draft report. In an e-mail received August 13, 2013, from State's GAO Liaison, State indicated that our report will inform its continuing work, mainly through its involvement in the JEMCO and JEMFAC. For example, State noted, the U.S. members of the JEMCO are currently taking steps to address decrement planning and improve the production of reliable indicator data in the compact priority sectors of health and education in the FSM. Similarly, the U.S. members of the JEMFAC continue to work with the RMI on its decrement plan.

Interior generally concurred with all five of our recommendations and briefly discussed each. With regard to our recommendations for actions involving JEMCO and JEMFAC, Interior noted examples of how it and other U.S. members of JEMCO and JEMFAC have worked to make improvements in the three areas mentioned in the recommendations: decrement plans, reliable indicator data to track progress in education and health, and addressing single audit findings. Interior also discussed our recommendations to determine, in consultation with grantor agencies, whether steps should be taken to improve accountability of noncompact funds to the FSM and RMI, including application of the high-risk designation for grant recipients. Interior noted that it cannot direct other agencies to take action with regard to any grant-specific issues and stated it was unaware of any precedent for federal agencies to jointly designate a grantee as high risk; however, Interior said it would discuss this approach with other federal agencies.

Although Interior also concurred with our final recommendation, to take actions to correct the disproportionate staffing shortage related to compact grant implementation and oversight, Interior's response indicates that it considers corrective action to be contingent on its receiving funding for new positions through the annual budget process. However, the intent of our recommendation is to have Interior work with its actual funding levels, whatever they may be, to correct what we observed to be a misalignment in how it allocates its staff. We found that compact grants account for the majority of grant funds that OIA administers and that OIA's staffing shortage has disproportionately affected compact grant oversight compared with other OIA activities. We believe it is feasible for OIA to address this imbalance regardless of whether it receives funding for new positions. Appendix IX presents a copy of the letter from Interior. Interior also provided technical comments that we incorporated in the report where appropriate.

In its written comments on our draft report, the FSM National Government focused on three areas of our reporting: (1) decrement planning, (2) data reliability issues for education and health indicators, and (3) financial accountability over compact and U.S. federal program funds. The FSM agreed on the importance of these three issues to the successful implementation of the amended compact. The FSM identified activities under way to plan for the decrement, such as the 2023 Planning Committee's efforts to identify ways to intensify private sector growth. Regarding data reliability, the FSM cited implementation of a contract to assess the national education system's ability to produce valid and reliable data and efforts under way to review the quality of health indicators with government staff. The FSM remarked on what it characterized as the heavy emphasis in our report of the possibility of achieving increased accountability over noncompact grant funds through a "high-risk" designation, but noted that it was assured because the process involved in a "high-risk" designation is not an arbitrary one. As some of the FSM's comments related to topics discussed at the August 22, 2013, JEMCO annual meeting, which we attended, we have updated our report to reflect information presented at that meeting. Appendix X presents a copy of the letter from the FSM National Government.

The government of the RMI also provided written comments on our draft report. The RMI believes it submitted adequate plans regarding the medium-term budget and investment framework and the decrement, while at the same time noting the usefulness of the decrement plan as a policy guide and planning tool, rather than as a mechanism for making line-item budgetary decisions. Regarding data reliability, the RMI generally agreed with our findings of data reliability problems in both the education and health sectors. The RMI agreed that there were limitations to their education data for certain indicators, and reported that they faced challenges in data collection due to the number of schools that were spread out over a large ocean area, and the deficient state of their transportation and communication systems. In the health sector, the RMI pointed out that it has 52 health centers spread throughout 29 atolls, making it difficult to collect data in a timely manner, and that it also lacks personnel dedicated solely to collecting and entering health indicator data. The RMI, however, noted that its Ministry of Health is seeking external assistance to improve health data. In response to our recommendation that—in order to improve financial accountability of noncompact U.S. grant assistance provided to the RMI—the Secretary of the Interior should consult with other agencies to determine whether the RMI meets the criteria to be designated as a high-risk grant recipient for noncompact funds, or whether other steps should be taken to improve accountability, the RMI noted that internal controls are now in place to detect and deter fraud, waste, and noncompliance with the fiscal procedures agreement or other U.S. federal regulations. For that reason, the RMI Ministry of Finance does not believe that any special conditions or restrictions for unsatisfactory performance or failure to comply with grant terms are warranted. As some of the RMI's comments related to topics discussed at the August 20, 2013, JEMFAC meeting, which we attended, we have updated our report to reflect information presented at that meeting. See appendix XI for a detailed presentation of comments from the RMI and our responses to them.

At both the annual JEMCO and JEMFAC meetings in August 2013, resolutions were passed in response to our recommendations related to decrement planning, data reliability, and addressing single audit findings. The resolutions approve the use of prior year unobligated funding to address one or more of the following three areas: (1) completing satisfactory plans to address annual decrements in compact funds, (2) producing reliable indicator data used to track progress in education and health, and (3) addressing all single audit findings in a timely manner.

In addition to providing copies of this report to your offices, we will send copies to interested congressional committees. We will also provide copies of this report to the Secretaries of the Interior, Education, HHS, and State, as well as to the President of the Federated States of Micronesia and the President of the Republic of the Marshall Islands. In addition, the report will be available at no charge on the GAO website at http://www.gao.gov.

If you or your staff have any questions regarding this report, please contact me at (202) 512-3149 or gootnickd@gao.gov. Contact points for our Offices of Congressional Relations and Public Affairs may be found on the last page of this report. GAO staff who made major contributions to this report are listed in appendix XII.

David Gootnick
Director, International Affairs and Trade

Appendix I: Objectives, Scope, and Methodology

This report examines, for fiscal years 2007 through 2011, (1) the Federated States of Micronesia's (FSM) and the Republic of the Marshall Islands' (RMI) use of compact funds in the education and health sectors; (2) the extent to which the FSM and RMI have made progress toward achieving their stated goals in education and health; and (3) the extent to which oversight activities by the FSM, RMI, and the United States ensure accountability for compact funding. In addition we provide information on the FSM and the RMI infrastructure sector grants.

To determine how the FSM and RMI used amended compact funds in the education and health sectors, we analyzed the single audits for the FSM National Government and the state governments of Chuuk and Pohnpei and for the RMI government for fiscal years 2007 through 2011. The single audits provide information on total education and health sector compact fund expenditures as well as total supplemental education grant expenditures in both countries and Ebeye special needs expenditures in the RMI. The single audits also provide details on specific expenditures within each of these sectors, such as personnel costs and medical supplies. However, data on specific expenditures for fiscal year 2007 and fiscal year 2008 were not available for the FSM National Government or the state of Chuuk; hence, we reported on specific sector expenditures for the FSM National Government, Chuuk, and Pohnpei for fiscal years 2009 through 2011 only. We were able, however, to provide specific expenditure data for the RMI for fiscal years 2007 through 2011. We report on the specific expenditures that constitute at least the top 80 percent of expenditures in the education and health sectors, as well as for supplemental education grant expenditures for both countries. Any remaining expenditure categories are aggregated under an "Other expenditures" category. Within the single audits, we also analyzed the total expenditures within the education and health sectors for the FSM National Government, Chuuk, Pohnpei, and the RMI government to determine the portion of sector expenditures supported by compact and noncompact U.S. funds. We determined that these data were sufficiently reliable for the purposes of our report.

To evaluate the extent to which the FSM and RMI made progress toward achieving their stated goals in the education and health sectors from fiscal years 2007 through 2011, we identified the indicators the FSM and RMI developed to track progress in those sectors. In assessing FSM progress, we used data from Chuuk and Pohnpei since these two states

represent 82 percent of the FSM population. As each country had
numerous indicators,[1] we selected a subset of the health and education
indicators in both countries to review. We used the U.S. 5-year reviews of
the FSM and RMI; Joint Economic Management Committee (JEMCO)
and Joint Economic Management and Financial Accountability Committee
(JEMFAC) health and education related resolutions from 2007 through
2012;[2] and the Millennium Development Goals (MDG) performance
measures as criteria to determine the subset of measures. We selected
these criteria for the following reasons: the U.S. 5-year reviews and the
JEMCO and JEMFAC resolutions identified indicators that reflected
country-specific concerns, while the MDG reflected global standards
because they were developed by international health and education
experts and agreed upon by almost all developing countries. An indicator
was selected to be part of the subset if it was included in two of the three
sources listed above for the FSM, and listed in all three sources for the
RMI. We also consulted with officials at the U.S. Departments of
Education (Education) and Health and Human Services (HHS) regarding
our proposed methodology. We then reviewed FSM and RMI annual
reports tracking these indicators for 2007 through 2011.[3] To determine
whether the data presented in the annual health and education indicator
reports were sufficiently reliable to measure progress in the compacts as
a whole, and in selected states, we reviewed the reports themselves,
reviewed JEMCO and JEMFAC resolutions related to health and
education data, and interviewed FSM and RMI officials responsible for
collecting and providing the data during our site visits in January 2013. In
the FSM and RMI, we also attempted to replicate the reported data in
some of the education and health reports. Additionally, we sent each
country a series of specific follow-up questions related to the subset of
indicators to learn more about each country's data collection and
verification activities, as well as to try to clarify discrepancies in the data
we identified. In some instances, the responses we obtained did not
provide sufficient information for us to determine that the data were

---

[1]The FSM and RMI both have 20 education indicators; the FSM has 14 health indicators
and the RMI has 26 health indicators.

[2]2012 JEMCO and JEMFAC resolutions were included because they had
recommendations pertaining to fiscal year 2011.

[3]For education-related reports, the data are for school years, and for health-related
reports, the data are for fiscal years.

reliable; in those instances we classified the indicators as "no basis to judge." We reported on the reliability of these indicators in the report.

To identify the extent to which the FSM and RMI governments conducted monitoring and oversight activities, we reviewed the amended compacts and fiscal procedures agreements to identify specific monitoring responsibilities. We also reviewed the U.S. briefing documents, as well as the minutes and resolutions, when available, related to the JEMCO and JEMFAC meetings. We further reviewed FSM and RMI documents—such as portfolios, quarterly performance reports, and annual reports, for fiscal years 2007-2011 as available—submitted by the FSM and RMI governments to the U.S. government to confirm compliance with accountability reporting requirements. We discussed the lack of required annual reporting with Department of the Interior (Interior) Office of Insular Affairs (OIA) officials. We obtained the single audit reports for the years 2006 through 2011 from the FSM Office of the National Auditor's website and the RMI's Office of the Auditor General. These reports included audits for the FSM National Government and the state governments of Chuuk and Pohnpei, and for the RMI government. In total, 24 single audit reports covered 6 years, a period that we considered sufficient for identifying common or persistent compliance and financial management problems involving U.S. funds (amended compact and other noncompact funds). We determined the timeliness of submission of the single audit reports by the insular area governments using the Federal Audit Clearinghouse's (FAC) "Form Date," which is the most recent date that the required SF-SAC data collection form[4] was received by the FAC. We did note that the "Form Date" is updated if a revised SF-SAC for that same fiscal year is subsequently filed. Our review of the contents of the single audit reports identified the auditors' opinions on the financial statements, matters cited by the auditors in their qualified opinions, the numbers of material weaknesses and reportable conditions reported by the auditors, and the status of corrective actions. We did not independently assess the quality of the audits or the reliability of the audit finding information. We analyzed the audit findings to determine if they had recurred in successive single audits and were still occurring in their most recent audit and categorized the auditor's opinions on the financial statements and the Schedules of Expenditures of Federal Awards.

---

[4]The FSM and RMI governments submit a data collection form (SF-SAC) that includes information about the auditee, its federal programs, and the results of the audit.

To determine oversight activities conducted by the OIA Honolulu office,
we reviewed senior management statements regarding the purpose and
function of this office and job descriptions for OIA staff. To identify the
staffing levels for the Honolulu office we reviewed Interior's 2010
workforce plan and obtained current staffing levels from OIA, as well as
reviewed Interior congressional budget submissions for 2013 and 2014
for actual staffing levels in 2011 and 2012. We discussed this information
with OIA officials to ensure that the data were sufficiently reliable for our
use.

To provide information on the FSM and RMI infrastructure sector grants,
we analyzed the single audits for the FSM National Government and the
state governments of Chuuk and Pohnpei and for the RMI government for
fiscal years 2007 through 2011. The single audits provide information on
total infrastructure sector compact fund expenditures and provide details
on specific expenditures within the infrastructure sector, such as
contractual services. However, data on specific expenditures for fiscal
year 2007 and fiscal year 2008 were not available for the FSM National
Government or the state of Chuuk; hence, we reported on specific sector
expenditures for the FSM National Government, Chuuk, and Pohnpei for
fiscal years 2009 through 2011 only. We were able, however, to provide
specific expenditure data for the RMI for fiscal years 2007 through 2011.
We report on the specific expenditures that constitute at least the top 80
percent of expenditures in the infrastructure sector. Any remaining
expenditure categories are aggregated under an "Other expenditures"
category. We determined that these data were sufficiently reliable for the
purposes of our report. We also reviewed the infrastructure development
and infrastructure maintenance plans for the FSM and RMI, interviewed
officials in the FSM and RMI project management units, and reviewed
progress reports submitted by the FSM and RMI. We reviewed JEMCO
and JEMFAC minutes and resolutions related to the infrastructure sector
and discussed the status of the infrastructure development plans and
projects with OIA's infrastructure grant manager. Additionally, we visited a
variety of ongoing completed projects in the FSM and RMI supporting the
health and education sectors in January 2013.

To address all objectives, we held interviews with officials from Interior
(Washington, D.C.; Honolulu, Hawaii; and the RMI) and the Department
of State (Washington, D.C.; the FSM; and the RMI). We also interviewed
officials from the HHS (Washington, D.C., and San Francisco, California)
and Education (Washington, D.C.). We traveled to the FSM (Chuuk and
Pohnpei) and the RMI (Kwajalein and Majuro Atolls) in January 2013. In
addition, in Chuuk state, we visited the islands of Fefen, Parem, Tonoas,

Udot, and Weno. In both countries we visited selected primary and
secondary schools, hospitals, and dispensaries. Our site selections were
judgmental because of the number of facilities on the islands, logistics,
and the time at our disposal. The facilities we visited exhibited a mix of
factors, such as facility type (elementary and secondary schools), age
(older and newer facilities), renovation status (those which had been
renovated and those that had not), and logistical needs. Where possible,
we selected facilities that we had visited in 2006 in order to draw
comparisons, to the degree possible. During our site visits we made
observations and performed spot checks. We used our 2006 report to
help select aspects to observe—such as cleanliness, electrical power,
and desks—and drug expiry dates to spot-check. These site visits were
not designed to yield generalizable conclusions but rather to illustrate
relevant conditions in the education and health sectors, including whether
there was functioning equipment, in both countries. We discussed
compact implementation with FSM (national, Chuuk, and Pohnpei
governments, as applicable) and RMI officials from the attorney general,
education, finance, foreign affairs, health, auditor general, public works,
and public service commission offices. Furthermore, we met with the
RMI's Office of Compact Implementation and Chief Secretary and the
FSM's Office of Statistics, Budget and Economic Management, Overseas
Development Assistance, and Compact Management. In Kwajalein Atoll,
we met Ebeye health and education officials to discuss compact
implementation issues. We also observed the 2012 annual meetings, the
2013 midyear meetings, and the 2013 annual meetings of the JEMCO
and the JEMFAC. We contacted Interior's Inspector General's Office in
Washington, D.C., to discuss ongoing investigations in the FSM and RMI;
however, we received no response to our inquiries.

We conducted this performance audit from August 2012 to September
2013 in accordance with generally accepted government auditing
standards. Those standards require that we plan and perform the audit to
obtain sufficient, appropriate evidence to provide a reasonable basis for
our findings and conclusions based on our audit objectives. We believe
that the evidence obtained provides a reasonable basis for our findings
and conclusions based on our audit objectives.

Appendix II: FSM and RMI Infrastructure Projects Related to Education and Health Sectors, Fiscal Years 2007–2011

FSM Infrastructure Projects

FSM Infrastructure Sector Compact Expenditures

In the infrastructure sector, the FSM spent the majority of sector compact funds, 74 percent, on contractual services, which include repairing and maintaining facilities such as schools (see fig. 7).

Figure 7: Federated States of Micronesia (FSM) Infrastructure Sector Expenditures, Fiscal Years 2009 through 2011

FSM infrastructure sector compact expenditures
Total, fiscal years 2009 through 2011: $41.7 million

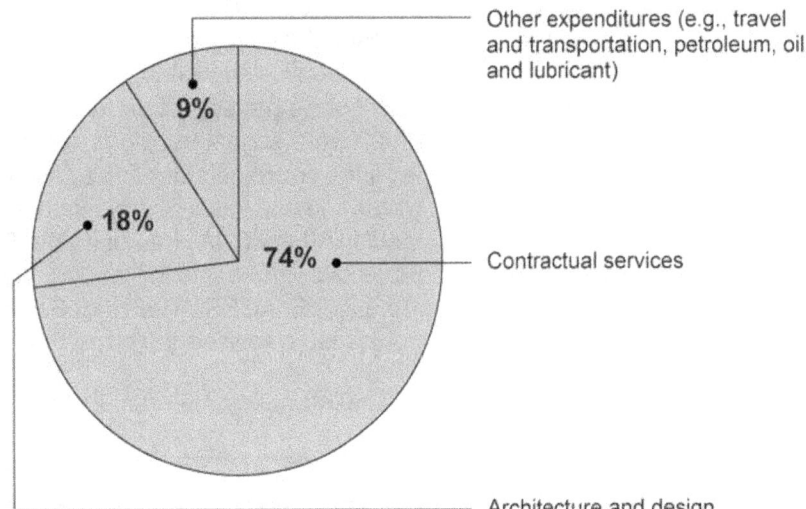

- Other expenditures (e.g., travel and transportation, petroleum, oil, and lubricant) — 9%
- Contractual services — 74%
- Architecture and design — 18%

Sources: GAO analysis based on information from FSM National Government, Chuuk, and Pohnpei single audit reports.

Note: Percentages may not add up to 100 due to rounding. Includes expenditures from the Infrastructure Maintenance Fund account, which is intended to finance the repair and maintenance of existing infrastructure.

FSM Tracked Infrastructure Project Completion

The FSM tracks progress in the infrastructure sector by the completion of projects. The FSM established an infrastructure development plan in 2004 and infrastructure maintenance funds by 2009.[1] As we reported in 2007, the infrastructure development plan proved to be problematic because it included synopses of 11 different infrastructure sectors, contained long lists of projects, and though its estimated costs were prepared by professional engineers, it did not provide explanations or support for individual projects or prioritize them as the Joint Economic Management Committee (JEMCO) required. Furthermore, the plan was not based on any type of assessment of the needs of specific areas in the FSM, did not meet with concurrence from the FSM states, and was not adopted by the FSM Congress.[2]

In fiscal year 2010, the FSM submitted an official list of priority infrastructure projects; JEMCO had already approved partial funding for 13 projects on the list at its September 2009 annual meeting.[3] Of the 19 priority-one projects, 4 were school buildings and classrooms in Pohnpei and 2 were school buildings in Yap; the remaining 13 were health-care facilities or projects directly affecting public health and safety, including water and wastewater projects and a detention center. The Office of Insular Affairs (OIA) has used the FSM's 2010 list of 19 priority-one projects as the basis for funding infrastructure projects in the FSM. As of June 2013, the FSM National Government and state governments had not issued a revised infrastructure development plan, according to OIA.[4]

---

[1]The amended compact established an infrastructure maintenance fund for the FSM National Government and the four state governments; it required that both the United States and the FSM governments contribute to the fund. However, the FSM governments have not consistently contributed their required share to the infrastructure maintenance funds. As a result, JEMCO required the FSM National Government to submit a deposit schedule of local cash contributions for the national government and each state government's infrastructure maintenance bank account, eliminating any unfunded liabilities by September 30, 2011.

[2]GAO, *Compacts of Free Association: Micronesia's and the Marshall Islands' Use of Sector Grants*, GAO-07-514R (Washington, D.C.: May 25, 2007).

[3]For the school and dispensary-related projects, JEMCO approval was for development of project scope, design, and construction bid package preparation. For the sanitation projects, JEMCO approval was for the preparation of preliminary engineering reports or development of preliminary cost estimates, or both.

[4]At its September 2010 meeting, JEMCO called for the FSM National and state governments to update its infrastructure development plan in fiscal year 2011, JEMCO Resolution 2010-8.

FSM infrastructure is overseen by a Program Management Unit (PMU) whose responsibilities include (1) certifying infrastructure projects, or determining that the scope and budget are reasonable and justifiable, and (2) ensuring that the projects will be designed to a professionally acceptable standard and that the project budgets properly reflect the costs of such as standard.[5] The PMU also certifies that projects in all four FSM states are consistent with the priorities listed in the FSM's infrastructure development plan. The PMU is to provide quarterly reports on construction activities to OIA. The reports generally include information related to the phase of a project, such as whether or not professional engineers and design services are being sought; the type of project (classroom, dispensaries, etc); the type of predesign document; whether or not a request for fee proposal was issued; and whether task orders were issued. PMU reports also include comments on such details as whether the estimated cost is higher than budgeted for, and whether land title documents were provided.

The FSM's PMU has not consistently provided quarterly progress reports on construction activities to OIA. According to OIA, significant delays, deficiencies, and project cost overruns have not been brought to OIA's attention in a timely manner as required by the amended compact's fiscal procedures agreement. OIA believes that the PMU's inability to ensure professional effectiveness on a continual basis through the services of an experienced Contracting Officer is hindering implementation of compact-funded infrastructure projects throughout the FSM.

In 2006, the FSM's PMU hired a Contracting Officer on behalf of the FSM National Government to execute project planning, design, and construction of projects throughout the FSM. Since 2006, the PMU has had a succession of Contracting Officers, eight in all. In a 2011 resolution, JEMCO stated that it would not consider approval of any new infrastructure project proposals until the PMU hired a professional Contracting Officer.[6] In December 2012, the PMU's Contracting Officer quit, claiming "constant interference from the FSM PMU Program Manager and a corrupted decision-making environment within the PMU

---

[5]Each state also has an entity responsible for providing oversight of infrastructure projects within the state.

[6]JEMCO Resolution 2011-6.

controlled by the PMU Program Manager." A new Contracting Officer was hired in February 2013.

FSM Progress in Building Schools Has Been Mixed, and Use of Maintenance Funds Is an Issue

During fiscal years 2007 through 2012, the FSM completed 6 education-related projects on the September 2009 JEMCO-approved list of 19 priority projects, and other projects are under way. A major factor in determining OIA's approval of a project has been whether the government holds clear title to the land.

- **Chuuk.** Land title disputes have been common in Chuuk, and as a result of this continuing problem, no new schools were built in Chuuk using infrastructure funds in fiscal years 2004 through 2011. However, according to OIA's infrastructure grant manager, because of the poor condition of schools in Chuuk, OIA permitted some school buildings to be renovated with infrastructure maintenance funds or carryover education sector grant funds, and these projects were not on the FSM list of priority infrastructure projects.[7] According to Chuuk's Planning and Statistics Office, six school projects have been completed on Weno and islands within the Chuuk lagoon using money from Chuuk's infrastructure maintenance fund.[8] According to the *Chuuk State: School Facility Repair and Construction Master Plan*, as of May 31, 2012, 51 primary schools and 5 secondary schools needed renovation, new construction, or both.

- **Pohnpei.** Land title issues have been less of a problem here, and 6 school projects were completed. Since 2009, classrooms were built at four elementary schools (a single project on the priority list), and buildings and classrooms were constructed at two high schools on the priority list.[9] Designs for two College of Micronesia facilities were

---

[7]According to OIA, it approved Chuuk's use of its infrastructure maintenance fund for this purpose because the new buildings replaced facilities at the schools that were unsafe and in poor condition. However, an OIA official noted it would not approve such use of the infrastructure maintenance funds again because the construction work funded in this instance was substandard.

[8]The school in Weno is Mwan Elementary School. In the lagoon islands, the schools are Nomusofo Junior High School, Southern Namoneas High School, Sino Elementary, Sapore Elementary, and West Fefen Elementary.

[9]The elementary schools are Kolonia, Nett, Saladak, and Sapwalap; the high schools are Pohnlangas (Madolenihmw) and Nanpei Memorial.

started but not completed for the Pohnpei State Campus, a vocational center and a learning resources center, according to OIA.[10]

FSM Progress in Building and Maintaining Health Facilities Has Been Limited

In the FSM, difficulty and delays in establishing JEMCO-approved priorities and unresolved land titling issues affected the construction and maintenance of health facilities. Dispensaries in Chuuk were on the OIA-approved list of FSM priority projects in fiscal year 2009, but these projects have not begun as of April 2013. Eight other projects with public health and safety aspects such as waterlines and sewers were also on the priority infrastructure project list; the majority of them are in Pohnpei.

In addition to approving the priority projects, JEMCO also approved funding for the repair of Pohnpei State Hospital's roof and ceiling.[11] The U.S. Army Humanitarian Assistance-FSM (HAFSM) Team completed the renovation project in 2013. HAFSM replaced the roof and undertook extensive internal repairs, including installing new dry wall and plumbing, as well as doing interior painting throughout the hospital. Repairs did not include the electrical system or air conditioning. Chuuk State Hospital was on the list of projects JEMCO approved in 2009 that got included in the 2010 list of 19 priority-one projects; however, it was not until June 2012 that the Chuuk state government's Infrastructure Planning and Implementation Committee finalized its revised infrastructure priorities in a plan that included a new hospital estimated to cost about $50 million dollars. The Chuuk plan also called for replacing 68 dispensaries in the outer islands using a common dispensary model estimated to cost $150,000 each. OIA had not received a plan from the national government to replace the dispensaries, as of June 2013.[12]

---

[10]JEMCO suspended compact funded design and associated engineering work for various College of Micronesia projects in 2010, pending approval of the college's restructuring plan by the Western Association of Schools and Colleges (JEMCO Resolution 2010-5). In fiscal year 2011, JEMCO decided that no College of Micronesia infrastructure projects would be considered for approval during fiscal years 2012 through 2016 (JEMCO Resolution 2011-2).

[11]JEMCO Resolutions 2010-6 and 2011-7.

[12]According to the FSM PMU, it has signed a contract to build 5 new dispensaries at a cost of approximately $298,400 each, a total cost of about $1.5 million.

RMI Infrastructure Projects

RMI Infrastructure Sector Compact Expenditures

In the infrastructure sector, the RMI spent the majority of compact sector funds, 65 percent, on capital outlay, which includes construction project and maintenance contracts payments for facilities such as schools and hospitals (see fig. 8).

Figure 8: Republic of the Marshall Islands (RMI) Infrastructure Sector Expenditures, Fiscal Years 2007 through 2011

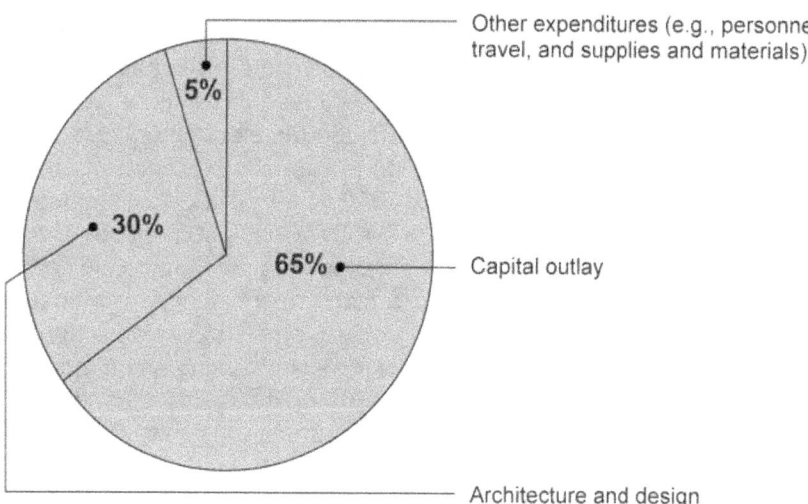

RMI infrastructure sector compact expenditures
Total, fiscal years 2007 through 2011: $68.6 million

Other expenditures (e.g., personnel, travel, and supplies and materials)

5%

30%

65% — Capital outlay

Architecture and design

Sources: GAO analysis based on information from RMI single audit reports.

Note: Includes expenditures from the Infrastructure Maintenance Fund account, which is intended to finance the repair and maintenance of existing infrastructure.

RMI Tracked Infrastructure Project Completion

The RMI tracks progress in the infrastructure sector by the completion of projects. The RMI expended $86.5 million dollars on infrastructure projects including infrastructure maintenance, from fiscal years 2004 through 2011, according to OIA.[13] The RMI stated it has constructed or

---

[13]This also includes $25 million dollars that went to projects at the College of the Marshall Islands.

renovated over 200 classroom facilities in the education sector and 45 projects in the health sector and has also conducted essential maintenance at its two hospitals.[14]

During fiscal years 2007 through 2011, the RMI's Project Management Unit was generally consistent in reporting monthly to the Office of Insular Affairs (OIA) on the status of construction activities, according to OIA. The reports included the project number and name as well as a brief description of the project. These reports also included categories such as the contract value, amount certified to date, estimated final cost, percentage completed, and completion date, and other details such project status—completed, on hold, or on-going for example.

In August 2012, allegations were raised by an RMI official regarding the Project Management Unit's use of substandard materials and bid rigging. OIA proposed a review by an independent engineering firm in response to the allegations. OIA recommended to the Joint Economic Management and Fiscal Accountability Committee (JEMFAC) at its March 2013 meeting that additional allocations of compact infrastructure funds to the RMI be withheld until the review was completed and the results submitted to JEMFAC. The RMI negotiated a contract with an independent professional engineering firm to undertake an assessment of the Project Management Unit's procedures, contract administration, and inspection process; the review is expected to commence in August 2013, according to OIA.

RMI Completed School and Health Facilities

The school buildings and dispensaries constructed throughout the RMI were built using standard designs prepared by a professional engineering firm. The College of the Marshall Islands Master Plan, initiated in 2007 with capital projects worth over $25 million, was almost completed when we visited in January 2013. Future infrastructure projects include the redevelopment plan for the hospital in Majuro. Various designs for the hospital project, which was estimated to cost between $50 million and $70 million, have been discussed for over 5 years. The key unresolved issue is the size of the new facility, which was still being discussed as of June 2013.

---

[14]The hospitals are in Majuro and Ebeye.

The RMI has recently begun to focus on preventive maintenance of infrastructure facilities. For example, in its fiscal year 2013 budget statement for infrastructure, the RMI noted that an adequate level of maintenance resources was critical for the longevity of the new College of the Marshall Islands campus, and RMI proposed allocating $280,000 for this purpose.

Appendix III: FSM and RMI Grant Assistance and Trust Fund Contributions under the Amended Compacts, Fiscal Years 2004–2023

Dollars in millions

Fiscal year	FSM grants (Section 211)	FSM trust fund (Sections 215 and 216)	RMI grants (Section 211)	RMI trust fund (Sections 216 and 217)
2004	$76.2	$16.0	$35.2	$7.0
2005	76.2	16.0	34.7	7.5
2006	76.2	16.0	34.2	8.0
2007	75.4	16.8	33.7	8.5
2008	74.6	17.6	33.2	9.0
2009	73.8	18.4	32.7	9.5
2010	73.0	19.2	32.2	10.0
2011	72.2	20.0	31.7	10.5
2012	71.4	20.8	31.2	11.0
2013	70.6	21.6	30.7	11.5
2014	69.8	22.4	32.2	12.0
2015	69.0	23.2	31.7	12.5
2016	68.2	24.0	31.2	13.0
2017	67.4	24.8	30.7	13.5
2018	66.6	25.6	30.2	14.0
2019	65.8	26.4	29.7	14.5
2020	65.0	27.2	29.2	15.0
2021	64.2	28.0	28.7	15.5
2022	63.4	28.8	28.2	16.0
2023	62.6	29.6	27.7	16.5

Source: Compacts of Free Association as Amended, Between the Government of the United States of America and the Government of the Federated States of Micronesia and the Government of the Republic of the Marshall Islands, Pub. L. No. 108-188.

Notes: Sections 211 of the amended compacts detail grant assistance to the FSM and the RMI, while Sections 215 and 216 of the U.S.–FSM compact and sections 216 and 217 of the U.S.–RMI compact detail contributions to the FSM and RMI trust funds. See Pub. L. No. 188-108, Dec. 17, 2003.

These dollar amounts shall be adjusted each fiscal year for inflation by the percentage that equals two-thirds of the percentage change in the U.S. gross domestic product implicit price deflator, or 5 percent, whichever is less in any one year, using the beginning of 2004 as a base. Grant funding can be fully adjusted for inflation after 2014, under certain U.S. inflation conditions.

The increase in RMI grant assistance from fiscal year 2013 to 2014 is due to a $2 million increase in payments to be made available for addressing the special needs of the community at Ebeye and other Marshallese communities within the Kwajalein Atoll.

Appendix IV: FSM and RMI Expenditures of U.S. Noncompact and Compact-Related Grant Funds, Fiscal Years 2007–2011

Table 6: Federated States of Micronesia (FSM) Expenditures of U.S. Noncompact and Compact-Related Grant Funds, Fiscal Years 2007 through 2011

Agency	Fiscal year					
	2007	2008	2009	2010	2011	Total
U.S. Department of Transportation	6,392,626	10,510,687	31,575,697	34,337,450	33,581,350	**116,397,810**
U.S. Department of Health and Human Services	5,171,983	5,603,314	6,492,503	8,767,750	7,668,872	**33,704,422**
U.S. Department of Education	4,696,968	4,119,530	4,620,678	3,916,819	3,692,482	**21,046,477**
U.S. Department of Homeland Security	4,306,572	3,738,391	1,605,349	1,001,751	1,405,026	**12,057,089**
U.S. Department of Commerce	1,096,129	1,218,474	1,277,555	1,360,272	1,401,309	**6,353,739**
U.S. Department of the Interior	2,082,664	976,180	935,753	713,596	767,784	**5,475,977**
U.S. Department of Agriculture	399,486	356,145	249,136	317,556	379,316	**1,701,639**
U.S. Department of Labor	517,558	0	0	0	0	**517,558**
U.S. Institute of Museum and Library Services	0	6,621	39,230	36,260	55,068	**137,179**
U.S. Small Business Administration	0	0	0	0	18,146	**18,146**
Total U.S. noncompact fund expenditures	24,663,986	26,529,342	46,795,901	50,451,454	48,969,353	**197,410,036**
Summary						
U.S. noncompact fund expenditures subtotal	**24,663,986**	**26,529,342**	**46,795,901**	**50,451,454**	**48,969,353**	197,410,036
U.S. compact funds expenditures subtotal	66,145,614	65,498,886	69,783,324	83,663,188	85,883,762	370,974,774
Total U.S. grant fund expenditures	**90,809,600**	**92,028,228**	**116,579,225**	**134,114,642**	**134,853,115**	**568,384,810**

Source: GAO analysis based on information from FSM National Government and Chuuk, Kosrae, Pohnpei, and Yap single audit reports.

Note: U.S. compact-related grant fund expenditures include energy, communications, and surveillance grant funds; sector grant funds; supplemental education grant funds; and funds that support the yearly single audits.

Table 7: Republic of the Marshall Islands (RMI) Expenditures of U.S. Noncompact and Compact-Related Grant Funds, Fiscal Years 2007 through 2011

Agency	Fiscal year					
	2007	2008	2009	2010	2011	Total
U.S. Department of Health and Human Services	4,358,210	3,550,420	3,968,212	5,504,080	4,956,471	**22,337,393**
U.S. Department of Education	3,459,510	2,277,950	2,109,783	1,878,145	1,871,736	**11,597,124**
U.S. Department of the Interior	1,328,436	1,854,303	1,292,051	1,436,710	1,378,192	**7,289,692**
U.S. Department of Agriculture	368,891	522,230	753,294	569,770	694,014	**2,908,199**
U.S. Department of Commerce	348,906	387,167	349,646	379,064	324,568	**1,789,351**
U.S. Small Business Administration	16,278	17,199	15,620	22,409	22,174	**93,680**
U.S. Department of Homeland Security	58,188	10,558	1,012	2,272	0	**72,030**
Total U.S. noncompact grant fund expenditures	9,938,419	8,619,827	8,489,618	9,792,450	9,247,155	**46,087,469**

Summary

	2007	2008	2009	2010	2011	Total
U.S. noncompact grant fund expenditures subtotal	**9,938,419**	**8,619,827**	**8,489,618**	**9,792,450**	**9,247,155**	**46,087,469**
U.S. compact-related grant fund expenditures subtotal	**56,640,580**	**53,669,271**	**59,876,574**	**57,572,450**	**89,876,922**	**317,635,797**
Total U.S. grant fund expenditures	**66,578,999**	**62,289,098**	**68,366,192**	**67,364,900**	**99,124,077**	**363,723,266**

Source: GAO analysis based on information from RMI single audit reports.

Note: U.S. compact-related grant fund expenditures include sector grant funds, supplemental education grant funds, landowners special needs grant funds, Kwajalein environment and landowners grant funds, and grant funds that support the yearly single audits.

Appendix V: Amended Compact Grant Allocations and Supplemental Education Grant Awards, Fiscal Years 2004–2013

From fiscal years 2004 through 2013, the U.S.–FSM Joint Economic Management Committee (JEMCO) and the U.S.–RMI Joint Economic Management and Financial Accountability Committee (JEMFAC) allocated about $1.1 billion in sector grants to the countries under the amended compacts. Additionally, about $142 million in supplemental education grant funds were provided to the countries during this period. Figures 9 and 10 show the distribution of allocations by sector for fiscal years 2004 through 2013 and tables 8 and 9 provide each country's allocation amounts, by sector, for this period.

Figure 9: U.S.–Federated States of Micronesia (FSM) Joint Economic Management Committee (JEMCO) Sector Allocations and Supplemental Education Grant Awards, Fiscal Year 2004 through Fiscal Year 2013

FSM JEMCO sector allocations and supplemental education grant awards (dollars in millions)

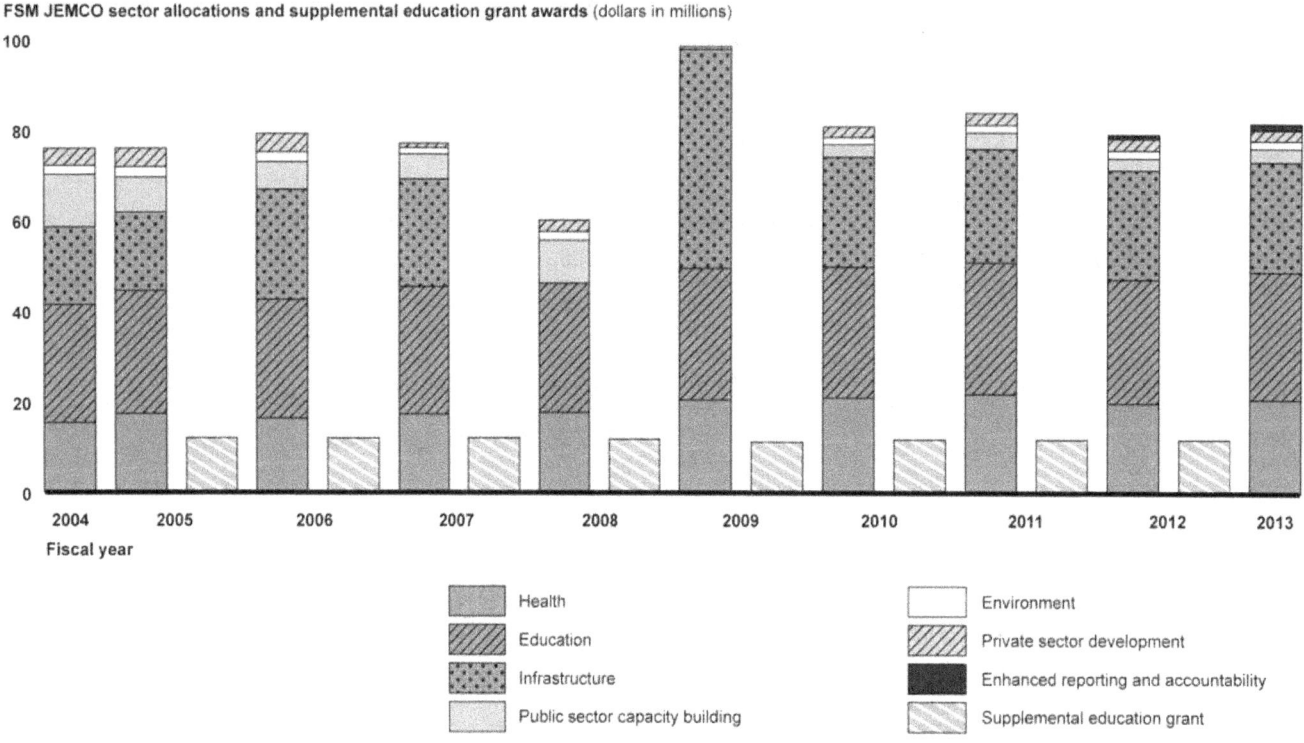

Sources: GAO analysis based on information from annual JEMCO resolutions, fiscal years 2004 through 2013.

Note: FSM allocations include data for the FSM National Government and the four states: Chuuk, Kosrae, Pohnpei, and Yap. Because the supplemental education grant funds lag by a year, the fiscal year 2004 funds were not awarded until fiscal year 2005, and the fiscal year 2013 funds will not be awarded until September 2013.

Table 8: U.S.–FSM Joint Economic Management Committee (JEMCO) Sector Allocations and Supplemental Education Grant Awards, Fiscal Years 2004 through 2013

Fiscal year	Sector	Amount (dollars)
2004	Health	15,443,116
	Education	25,965,572
	Infrastructure	17,119,155
	Public sector capacity building	11,662,846
	Environment	2,023,192
	Private sector development	3,786,119
	Total sector allocations	**76,000,000**
	Supplemental education grant	0
2005	Health	17,430,733
	Education	27,105,047
	Infrastructure	17,249,121
	Public sector capacity building	7,786,238
	Environment	2,389,951
	Private sector development	4,038,910
	Total sector allocations	**76,000,000**
	Supplemental education grant	12,083,360
2006	Health	16,394,939
	Education	26,132,059
	Infrastructure	24,335,718
	Public sector capacity building	6,175,914
	Environment	2,137,452
	Private sector development	4,039,163
	Total sector allocations	**79,215,245**
	Supplemental education grant	12,059,401
2007	Health	17,309,531
	Education	28,051,609
	Infrastructure	23,753,270
	Public sector capacity building	5,609,691
	Environment	1,408,631
	Private sector development	1,011,048
	Total sector allocations	**77,143,780**
	Supplemental education grant	12,010,680
2008	Health	17,741,499
	Education	28,423,788
	Infrastructure	0

Fiscal year	Sector	Amount (dollars)
	Public sector capacity building	9,505,422
	Environment	1,889,943
	Private sector development	2,506,345
	Total sector allocations	**60,066,997**
	Supplemental education grant	11,790,855
2009	Health	20,482,050
	Education	29,013,338
	Infrastructure	48,428,760
	Public sector capacity building	600,000
	Environment	0
	Private sector development	0
	Total sector allocations	**98,524,148**
	Supplemental education grant	11,204,790
2010	Health	21,007,869
	Education	28,774,255
	Infrastructure	24,303,552
	Public sector capacity building	2,887,816
	Environment	1,579,510
	Private sector development	2,333,638
	Total sector allocations	**80,886,640**
	Supplemental education grant	11,791,333
2011	Health	21,925,919
	Education	28,893,733
	Infrastructure	25,086,084
	Public sector capacity building	3,764,219
	Environment	1,659,867
	Private sector development	2,618,701
	Total sector allocations	**83,948,523**
	Supplemental education grant	11,766,573
2012	Health	19,799,593
	Education	27,229,001
	Infrastructure	24,222,240
	Public sector capacity building	2,661,097
	Environment	1,752,226
	Private sector development	2,580,211
	Enhanced reporting and accountability	908,830
	Total sector allocations	**79,153,198**

Fiscal year	Sector	Amount (dollars)
	Supplemental education grant	11,751,632
2013	Health	20,692,562
	Education	28,034,838
	Infrastructure	24,437,952
	Public sector capacity building	2,946,227
	Environment	1,718,017
	Private sector development	2,373,494
	Enhanced reporting and accountability	1,481,237
	Total sector allocations	**81,684,327**
	Supplemental education grant	0

Sources: GAO analysis based on information from annual JEMCO resolutions, fiscal years 2004 through 2013.

Notes: Allocations may differ from actual grant awards. Because the supplemental education grant funds lag by a year, the fiscal year 2004 funds were not awarded until fiscal year 2005, and the fiscal year 2013 funds will not be awarded until September 2013.

Figure 10: U.S.–RMI Joint Economic Management and Financial Accountability Committee (JEMFAC) Sector Allocations and Supplemental Education Grant Awards, Fiscal Year 2004 through Fiscal Year 2013

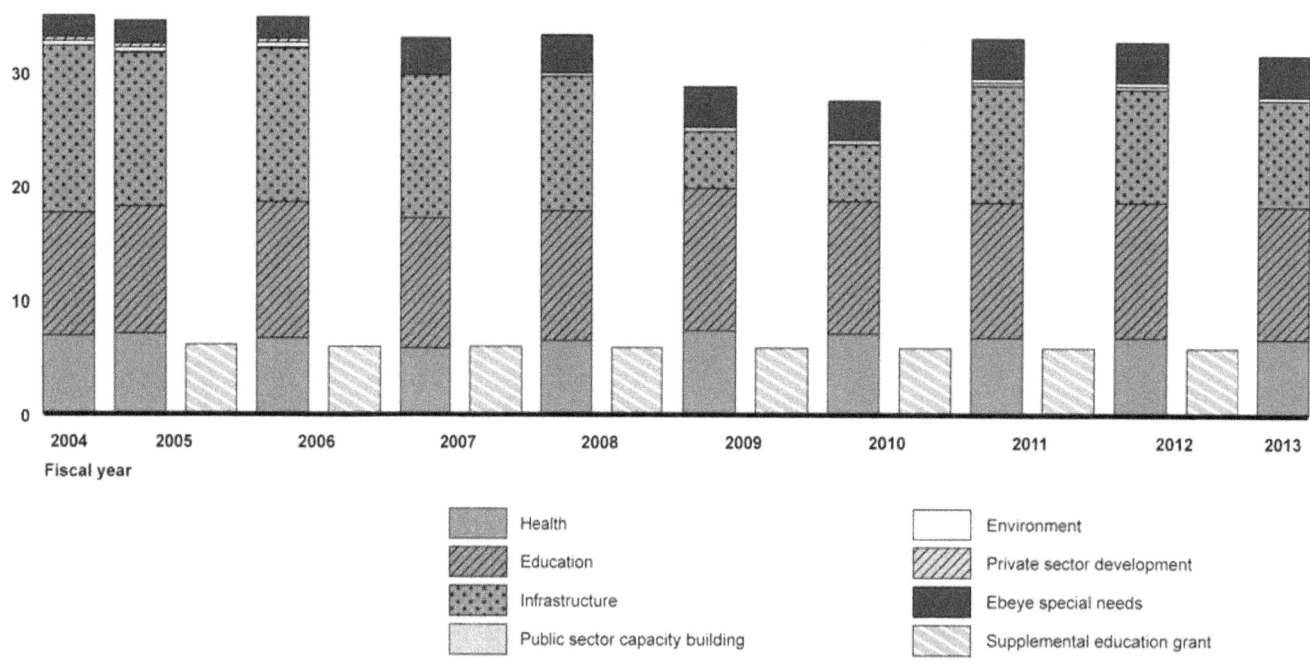

RMI JEMFAC sector allocations and supplemental education grant awards (dollars in millions)

Health	Environment
Education	Private sector development
Infrastructure	Ebeye special needs
Public sector capacity building	Supplemental education grant

Sources: GAO analysis based on information from annual JEMFAC resolutions, fiscal years 2004 through 2013.

Note: Because the supplemental education grant funds lag by a year, the fiscal year 2004 funds were not awarded until fiscal year 2005, and the fiscal year 2013 funds will not be awarded until September 2013.

Table 9: U.S.–RMI Joint Economic Management and Financial Accountability Committee (JEMFAC) Sector Allocations and Supplemental Education Grant Awards, Fiscal Years 2004 through 2013

Fiscal year	Sector	Amount (dollars)
2004	Health	6,894,448
	Education	10,748,932
	Infrastructure	14,700,000
	Public sector capacity building	0
	Environment	400,000
	Private sector development	356,620
	Ebeye Special Needs	1,900,000
	Total sector allocations	**35,000,000**
	Supplemental education grant	0
2005	Health	7,064,097
	Education	11,141,921
	Infrastructure	13,485,745
	Public sector capacity building	103,514
	Environment	404,720
	Private sector development	361,943
	Ebeye Special Needs	1,992,420
	Total sector allocations	**34,554,360**
	Supplemental education grant	6,100,000
2006	Health	6,682,741
	Education	11,934,083
	Infrastructure	13,495,679
	Public sector capacity building	103,514
	Environment	408,000
	Private sector development	361,943
	Ebeye Special Needs	1,882,440
	Total sector allocations	**34,868,400**
	Supplemental education grant	5,941,769
2007	Health	5,815,108
	Education	11,408,682
	Infrastructure	12,573,085
	Public sector capacity building	0
	Environment	0
	Private sector development	0

Fiscal year	Sector	Amount (dollars)
	Ebeye Special Needs	3,263,969
	Total sector allocations	**33,060,844**
	Supplemental education grant	5,990,490
2008	Health	6,512,349
	Education	11,336,978
	Infrastructure	11,855,213
	Public sector capacity building	300,000
	Environment	0
	Private sector development	0
	Ebeye Special Needs	3,345,830
	Total sector allocations	**33,350,370**
	Supplemental education grant	5,895,668
2009	Health	7,404,620
	Education	12,457,410
	Infrastructure	5,000,000
	Public sector capacity building	425,000
	Environment	0
	Private sector development	0
	Ebeye Special Needs	3,536,134
	Total sector allocations	**28,823,164**
	Supplemental education grant	5,886,017
2010	Health	7,159,858
	Education	11,600,728
	Infrastructure	5,000,000
	Public sector capacity building	413,380
	Environment	0
	Private sector development	0
	Ebeye Special Needs	3,451,055
	Total sector allocations	**27,625,021**
	Supplemental education grant	5,895,667
2011	Health	6,834,858
	Education	11,839,151
	Infrastructure	10,296,314
	Public sector capacity building	300,000
	Environment	325,000
	Private sector development	0

Fiscal year	Sector	Amount (dollars)
	Ebeye Special Needs	3,486,781
	Total sector allocations	**33,082,104**
	Supplemental education grant	5,895,667
2012	Health	6,834,858
	Education	11,839,151
	Infrastructure	9,958,191
	Public sector capacity building	300,000
	Environment	325,000
	Private sector development	0
	Ebeye Special Needs	3,515,400
	Total sector allocations	**32,772,600**
	Supplemental education grant	5,885,052
2013	Health	6,693,788
	Education	11,598,952
	Infrastructure	9,406,891
	Public sector capacity building	0
	Environment	325,000
	Private sector development	0
	Ebeye Special Needs	3,587,010
	Total sector allocations	**31,611,641**
	Supplemental education grant	-

Sources: GAO analysis based on information from annual JEMFAC resolutions, fiscal years 2004 through 2013.

Notes: Allocations may differ from actual grant awards. Because the supplemental education grant funds lag by a year, the fiscal year 2004 funds were not awarded until fiscal year 2005, and the fiscal year 2013 funds will not be awarded until September 2013.

As shown in figures 11 and 12, the education, health, and infrastructure sectors in both countries received the most funding during this period, consistent with provisions in the amended compacts legislation indicating that these sectors were priorities.

Figure 11: Federated States of Micronesia (FSM) Total Sector Allocations and Percentages, Fiscal Years 2004 through 2013

FSM sector allocations

Total, fiscal years 2004 through 2013: $792.6

(dollars in millions)

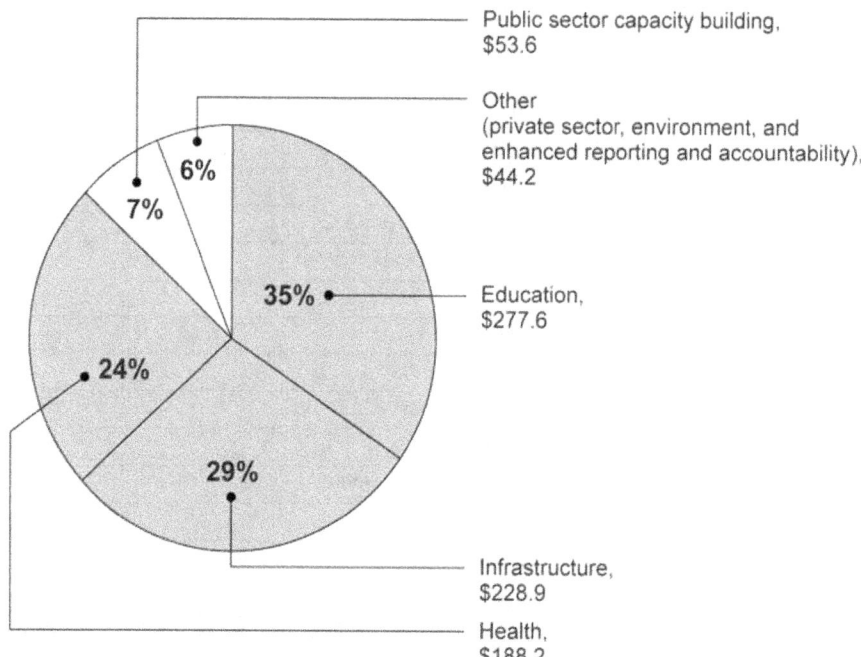

Public sector capacity building, $53.6

Other (private sector, environment, and enhanced reporting and accountability), $44.2

Education, $277.6

Infrastructure, $228.9

Health, $188.2

Sources: Annual JEMCO resolutions, fiscal years 2004 through 2013.

Notes: Percentages may not add up to 100 due to rounding. Sum of sector allocations may not add up to the total due to rounding. Supplemental education grant funds are not included in this figure.

Figure 12: Republic of the Marshall Islands (RMI) Total Sector Allocations and Percentages, Fiscal Years 2004 through 2013

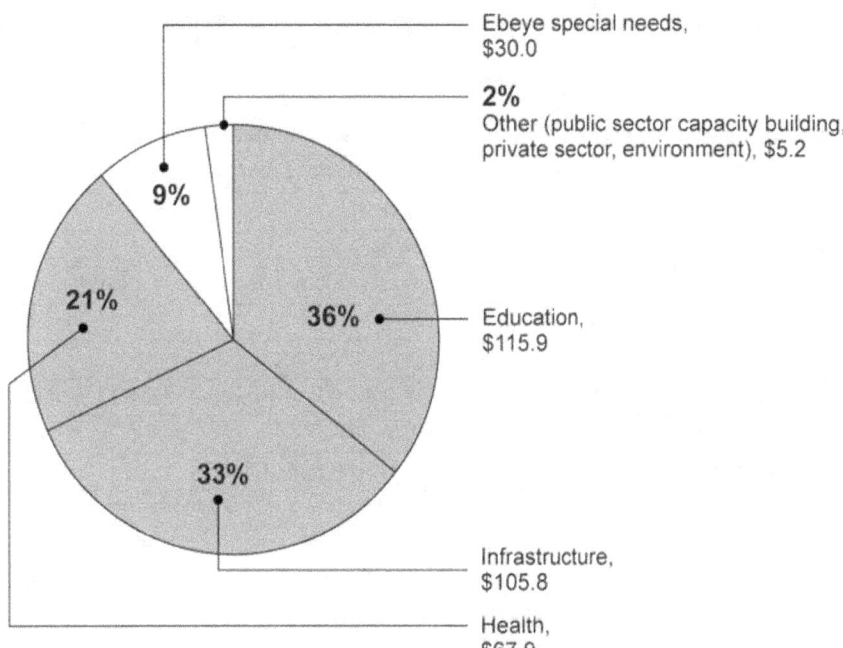

RMI sector allocations

Total, fiscal years 2004 through 2013: $324.7

(dollars in millions)

Ebeye special needs, $30.0

2%
Other (public sector capacity building, private sector, environment), $5.2

Education, $115.9

Infrastructure, $105.8

Health, $67.9

Sources: Annual JEMFAC resolutions, fiscal years 2004 through 2013.

Notes: Percentages may not add up to 100 due to rounding. Sum of sector allocations may not add up to the total due to rounding. Supplemental education grant funds are not included in this figure.

Appendix VI: Education and Health Indicators for the FSM and the RMI, Fiscal Years 2007–2011

Tables 10 and 11 list the education and health indicators that the Federated States of Micronesia (FSM) tracked during fiscal years 2007 through 2011. Tables 12 and 13 list the education and health indicators that the Republic of the Marshall Islands (RMI) tracked during the same period.

Table 10: Federated States of Micronesia (FSM) Education Indicators, Fiscal Years 2007 through 2011

1.	Student enrollment by grade level and gender
2.	Completion/graduation rate for 8th and 12th grades (private and public)
3.	Number of schools by grade level (elementary and secondary)
4.	Number of schools by size (based on enrollment)
5.	Number of schools operating half-day sessions
6.	Number and percent of staff by education level (diploma, associate of arts degree, etc.)
7.	Number of teachers/staff by grade level
8.	Average daily student attendance rate by grade level and gender
9.	Base populations by school age groups (i.e., total no. of 4-5 year olds, 6-13 year olds, 14-18, etc.)
10.	Student-to-teacher ratio (private and public)
11.	Percent of base school-age population in school by age groups
12.	Drop-out rate by grade level and gender (use beginning and ending enrollment)
13.	Number and percent of grade completers going to high school and high school graduates going to higher education
14.	Number and percent of student achieving "Proficiency" level and above, at selected grade levels for standardized tests (e.g., SAT) or criterion-referenced tests (e.g., locally developed tests)
15.	Number of student textbooks by subject areas and grade levels
16.	Per pupil expenditure (annual or entire operating K-12 budget divided by enrolled student count)
17.	Number of parent involvement activities per year by school and average number of parents participating
18.	Student enrollment in local institutions of higher education
19.	Number of institutions of higher education graduates by diploma/degree level
20.	Average teacher attendance rate by grade level (elementary and secondary)
21.	Scholarships[a]

Source: Federated States of Micronesia: JEMCO 20 Education Indicators Report.

[a]This indicator was added in 2011. During the time frame of our review, fiscal years 2007 through 2011, there were 20 indicators, with the exception of 2011. For the purposes of this report, we refer to the FSM as having 20 education indicators; even the 2011 JEMCO report tracking the education data does this in its title, JEMCO 20 Education Indicators Report.

Table 11: Federated States of Micronesia (FSM) Health Indicators, Fiscal Years 2007 through 2011

1.	Infant mortality rate is reduced to less than 16/1000 by 2015
2.	Immunization coverage of 2 year old children is increased to not less than 90% by year 2015
3.	Mental illness is reduced (indicator: rate of completed suicide reduced to 10% by 2015)
4.	At least 70% of 3rd graders received sealant by 2015 (2004 Baseline)
5.	The average length of hospital stay is less than 7 days for each State Hospital by 2015
6.	Off-island medical referral costs in all states reduce to less than 10% of total health sector expenditures by 2015
7.	Essential drugs and supplies available (indicators: ORS, combo OCP, Amox, IV, chloramphenicol, glyburide, ethanol, and HCTZ) all in stock 80% of days)
8.	The number of individuals enrolled under a health insurance plan is increased 10% by 2015
9.	Quality Assurance Systems Functioning (indicator: quarterly audits and improvement plans, based on written policy and procedure standards, are produced for specific areas in each state's hospitals)
10.	Decentralize primary care services—number of encounters provided in homes and dispensaries will increase 20% by 2015
11.	Decentralize primary care services—number of patient encounters at hospitals' clinics will decrease by 10% by 2015
12.	Biomedical equipment is functional (indicator: Na+ K+ ALT, Bili, and Creatinin all available 80% of days)
13.	Reduce incidence of diarrheal diseases by 10% by 2015
14.	Noncommunicable diseases control (indicator: reduce the incidence of diabetic hospitalization by 10% in 2015)

Source: Federated States of Micronesia, Department of Health and Social Affairs, Fourteen Health Indicators Report: 2004-2015.

Table 12: Republic of the Marshall Islands (RMI) Education Indicators, Fiscal Years 2007 through 2011

1.	Total enrollment by grade and gender
2.	Completion/Graduation rate for 8th and 12th grade
3.	Number of schools by grade level
4.	Number of schools by enrollment size (primary and secondary)
5.	Number of schools operating half-day sessions
6.	Number and percent of teachers by education level (related to teacher certification and training)
7.	Number of teacher/staff by grade level
8.	Average daily attendance
9.	Base population of school age groups
10.	Student/teacher ratio by geographic area/all schools
11.	Percent of base-school-age population in school by age group
12.	Drop out rate by grade level and gender
13.	Number/percent of 8th-grade completers going to high school
14.	Marshall Islands Standard Assessment Test (grades 3, 6,8) % student benchmark scores at "proficient and above"
15.	Number of students textbooks by subject areas and grade level
16.	Per pupil expenditure
17.	Number of parent involvement activities per year by school

18. Student enrollment in local institution of higher education (RMI-USP Joint Education Program)a
19. Number of higher education graduates by diploma/degree
20. Number of staff full time

Source: Republic of the Marshall Islands, Ministry of Education, Portfolio Budget Statements.

Note: The RMI-USP Joint Education Program is a partnership in education between the RMI and the University of the South Pacific (USP). The joint program includes both a preliminary program and a subsequent foundation program; enrollment data reported here include enrollment in both the preliminary and foundation programs.

Table 13: Republic of the Marshall Islands Health (RMI) Indicators, Fiscal Years 2007 through 2011

1. Reduce infant mortality rate by 50% from 2004-2015/1000 live births
2. Increase immunization coverage to 95% by 2015 for 2-year-olds
3. Increase percent of total immunization coverage levels for adolescent and adults to 95% by 2015
4. Reduce cases of suicide by half by 2015
5. Improve access to dental services
6. Reduce the prevalence of cancers by 2015 by 16% per 100,000 population
7. Reduce the average length of hospital stay (days)
8. Decrease in number of referrals
9. Maintain maternal mortality ratio at <1/100,000 by 2015
10. Reduce child mortality rate by 60% from 2004 to 2015 *100,000
11. Reduce mortality rate for tuberculosis to <1/100,000 by 2015
12. Reduce the prevalence of tuberculosis by <1/100,000 by 2015
13. Reduce the prevalence of teenage pregnancy by 75% by 2015 per 100,000
14. Reduce the prevalence of HIV/STI in age 15-49 to <1/100,000 by 2015
15. Reduce the prevalence of diabetes by 16% by 2015
16. Reduce diabetes related cause of death (mortality rate by 10%)
17. Eliminate leprosy by 2010 to < 1/100,000 (country goal)
18. Reduce the diseases specific mortality rate from malnutrition by 100% from 2004 to 2015
19. Eliminate the prevalence of malnutrition in children < 5 years old from 2004 to 2015 per 100,000
20. Reduce prevalence of water borne diseases by 2015
21. Reduce the prevalence of acute rheumatic (valvular) heart diseases to 1/100,000 by 2015
22. Reduce the prevalence of noncommunicable disease by 10% by 2015 (100,000)
23. Reduce the incidence of alcohol- and substance-related injuries
24. Health-awareness activities conducted
25. Disease surveillance (lab service)
26. School-based health public on Ebeye

Source: Republic of the Marshall Islands, Ministry of Health, Overarching Health Measures.

Appendix VII: Single Audit Reports for the FSM and the RMI, Fiscal Years 2006–2011

The National Government of the Federated States of Micronesia (FSM) and the individual FSM states (Chuuk and Pohnpei)[1] submitted their required single audit reports on time for 5 of the 6 fiscal years from 2006 through 2011. Similarly, the Republic of the Marshall Islands (RMI) submitted its single audit reports on time during those years except for fiscal year 2011. Half of the financial statement audit opinions for the FSM and all for the RMI were unqualified for fiscal years 2006 through 2011.[2] However, 17 of 18 financial statement audits for those years from the FSM and all 6 from the RMI found material weaknesses and significant deficiencies resulting in the entities receiving qualified audit opinions[3] with regard to internal controls over financial reporting. In most of the single audit reports submitted by both countries for those years, auditors also rendered qualified audit opinions on compliance with requirements of major federal programs. In addition, our review of the single audit reports found that internal control weaknesses have persisted in both countries since we last reported on their single audits in December 2006. As a result of persistent weaknesses in RMI's single audit reports, in March 2013, the Department of the Interior's Office of Insular Affairs (OIA) recommended to the U.S.–RMI Joint Economic Management and Financial Accountability Committee (JEMFAC) that it refrain from allocating unexpended grant funds from fiscal year 2011 and fiscal year 2012 until the RMI demonstrated that it had resolved all current questioned costs.

---

[1]In the FSM, we focused our review on the National Government and the state governments of Chuuk and Pohnpei. We did not include in our review the state governments of Yap and Kosrae. See app. I for additional discussion of scope.

[2]An unqualified opinion is given when the auditor is reasonably assured that the financial statements are free of material misstatements.

[3]A qualified opinion is given when the auditor finds conditions such as a lack of supporting evidence or a restriction on the scope of the audit.

Single Audits Are Key Control for Oversight and Monitoring

The amended compacts and their respective fiscal procedures agreements require the FSM and RMI to submit reports each year on audits conducted within the meaning of the Single Audit Act, as amended.[4] Single audits generally cover the entire organization and focus on recipients' internal controls over financial reporting and compliance with laws and regulations governing federal awards. A single audit report includes the following:

- the auditor's opinion (or disclaimer of opinion, as appropriate) regarding whether the financial statements are presented fairly in all material respects in conformity with generally accepted accounting principles, and a report on internal controls related to financial statements;
- the entity's audited financial statements;
- the schedule of expenditures of federal awards and the auditor's opinion on whether the schedule is reported fairly in relation to the financial statements as a whole;
- the auditor's opinion (or disclaimer of opinion) regarding whether the auditee complied with the laws, regulations, and provisions of contracts and grant agreements (such as the compact), which could have a direct and material effect on each major federal program, and a report on findings on internal controls related to federal programs;
- a summary of findings and any questioned costs for the federal program; and
- corrective action plans for findings identified for the current year as well as unresolved findings from prior fiscal years.

Single audits are a key control for the oversight and monitoring of the FSM and RMI governments' use of U.S. awards, and the resulting audit reports are due at the Federal Audit Clearinghouse—which includes an automated public database of single audit information on the Internet—9

---

[4]All nonfederal entities that expend $500,000 or more of federal awards in a year are required to obtain an annual audit in accordance with the Single Audit Act, as amended. 31 U.S.C. § 7501 et seq.

months after the end of the audited period.[5] For the FSM and RMI, that is by July 1 each year. All single audit reports include the auditor's opinion on the audited financial statements and a report on the internal controls related to financial reporting.

Timeliness of Submission: Both Countries Submitted Their Single Audit Reports on Time for 5 of the 6 Years Reviewed

The FSM National Government and Chuuk state submitted their single audit reports late for fiscal year 2006 but submitted them on time for fiscal years 2007 through 2011. The RMI submitted its single audit report on time for fiscal years 2006 through 2010 but submitted its report late for fiscal year 2011. Table 14 shows the timeliness of reports for the FSM and the RMI.[6]

[5]The fiscal procedures agreements specify that the audits are due 6 months after the fiscal year ends, but the Department of the Interior (Interior) believes that the time frame of 6 months was a mistake in the agreements. According to Interior officials, they have allowed the countries 9 months, which is generally the required time frame under the Single Audit Act. According to the act, there is generally no standard due date for the annual single audit. The audited entity, upon hiring the auditor, negotiates a due date for the audit within 9 months after the close of the entity's fiscal year. The entity must have time to read the report and prepare the corrective action plan that is required to be included in the reporting package.

[6]Although not included in the scope of this report, the FSM National Government and Chuuk and Pohnpei state governments submitted their 2012 single audit reports on time; the RMI government did not.

Table 14: Number of Months Single Audits from the Federated States of Micronesia (FSM) and the Republic of the Marshall Islands (RMI) Were Received Past Their Deadline, by Country and State, Fiscal Years 2006 through 2011

Fiscal year	FSM National Government	Chuuk state	Pohnpei state	RMI
2006	2[a]	2	0	0
2007	0	0	0	0
2008	0	0	0	0
2009	0	0	0	0
2010	0	0	0	0
2011	0	0	0	8

Sources: GAO analysis of Office of Management and Budget Circular A-133, single audit reports, and Federal Audit Clearinghouse submission dates.

Notes: The deadline is 9 months after the close of the entity's fiscal year. To determine whether reports were submitted late and, if so, by how many months, we compared the deadline for each report with its most recent submission date for the required Single Audit form in the Federal Audit Clearinghouse database.

[a]The FSM National Government's single audit cannot be completed until the states' single audits have been completed. Thus, if any state is late, the FSM National Government's audit will also be late. Chuuk submitted its 2006 single audit late.

In 2011, FSM, except for Chuuk State, and RMI Received Unqualified Opinions on Their Financial Statements

Among the 24 audit reports submitted by the FSM national and two state governments and by the RMI for fiscal years 2006 through 2011, 15 reports received unqualified opinions. For fiscal years 2006 through 2008, the FSM National Government received qualified opinions on their financial statements. However, the FSM National Government improved its financial management reporting and received an unqualified ("clean") audit opinion on its financial statements for fiscal years 2009 through 2011. In 2006, Chuuk received a disclaimer of opinion, which is given when the auditor determines that the audit cannot be completed in accordance with generally accepted auditing standards and therefore an opinion cannot be expressed on the financial statements. For fiscal years 2007 through 2011, Chuuk received qualified opinions on its financial statements. Chuuk's 2011 financial statement audit opinion was qualified because the financial statements did not report a liability for land leases and related claims payable in the governmental activities and general fund or the expenditure for the current period reflecting the change in that liability. Table 15 shows the type of financial statement audit opinions for the FSM and the RMI for fiscal years 2006 through 2011.

Table 15: Financial Statement Audit Opinions for the Federated States of Micronesia (FSM) and the Republic of the Marshall Islands (RMI), Fiscal Years 2006 through 2011

Year	Type of Opinion			
	FSM National Government	Chuuk state	Pohnpei state	RMI
2006	Qualified	Disclaimer	Unqualified	Unqualified[a]
2007	Qualified	Qualified	Unqualified	Unqualified
2008	Qualified	Qualified	Unqualified	Unqualified
2009	Unqualified	Qualified	Unqualified	Unqualified
2010	Unqualified	Qualified	Unqualified	Unqualified
2011	Unqualified	Qualified	Unqualified	Unqualified

Source: GAO analysis of FSM and RMI single audit reports.

[a]The Independent Auditors' Report on the financial statements of the governmental activities, each major fund, and the aggregate remaining fund information, expressed an unqualified opinion and an adverse opinion on the financial statement of the aggregate discretely presented components units due to the omission of the Kwajalein Atoll Joint Utilities Resources Inc. and the inability of Air Marshall Islands Inc. to produce audited financial statements.

All RMI and FSM Audits Found Material Weaknesses, or Significant Deficiencies, or Both, Relating to Internal Control over Financial Reporting and Compliance with Federal Programs

For fiscal years 2006 through 2011, 17 of 18 financial statement audits from the FSM National Government and the two FSM states and all 6 from the RMI found material weaknesses,[7] significant deficiencies,[8] or both in internal control over (1) financial reporting and (2) compliance with the requirements of major federal awards. (For a detailed count of these reportable findings, see table 16 for the FSM and table 17 for the RMI.)

[7]American Institute of Certified Public Accountants, Statement on Auditing Standard No. 115, "Communicating Internal Control Related Matters Identified in an Audit," states that a material weakness is a deficiency, or a combination of deficiencies, in internal control such that there is a reasonable possibility that a material misstatement of the entity's financial statements will not be prevented, or detected and corrected on a timely basis. A deficiency in internal control exists when the design or operation of a control does not allow management or employees, in the normal course of performing their assigned functions, to prevent, or detect and correct misstatements on a timely basis.

[8]American Institute of Certified Public Accountants, Statement on Auditing Standard No. 115, "Communicating Internal Control Related Matters Identified in an Audit," states that a significant deficiency is a deficiency, or a combination of deficiencies, in internal control that is less severe than a material weakness, yet important enough to merit attention by those charged with governance.

Table 16: Number of Material Weaknesses and Significant Deficiencies Reported in Single Audit Reports for the Federated States of Micronesia (FSM) National Government and States, Fiscal Years 2006 through 2011

		Reportable findings on internal control over financial reporting			Reportable findings on internal control over compliance with federal awards		
		Material weaknesses	Significant deficiencies	Total	Material weaknesses	Significant deficiencies	Total
2006	FSM National Government[a]	3	9	12	1	16	17
	Chuuk	18	0	18	14	0	14
	Pohnpei	0	0	0	0	6	6
	Total	**21**	**9**	**30**	**15**	**22**	**37**
2007	FSM National Government[a]	14	0	14	0	14	14
	Chuuk	8	4	12	5	0	5
	Pohnpei	0	1	1	0	4	4
	Total	**22**	**5**	**27**	**5**	**18**	**23**
2008	FSM National Government[a]	6	0	6	7	7	14
	Chuuk	3	0	3	1	0	1
	Pohnpei	0	1	1	0	2	2
	Total	**9**	**1**	**10**	**8**	**9**	**17**
2009	FSM National Government[a]	5	0	5	10	10	20
	Chuuk	3	0	3	2	0	2
	Pohnpei	0	1	1	0	1	1
	Total	**8**	**1**	**9**	**12**	**11**	**23**
2010	FSM National Government[a]	7	1	8	11	1	12
	Chuuk	1	0	1	1	0	1
	Pohnpei	0	1	1	0	1	1
	Total	**8**	**2**	**10**	**12**	**2**	**14**
2011	FSM National Government[a]	4	3	7	4	8	12
	Chuuk	3	2	5	0	1	1
	Pohnpei	0	1	1	0	1	1
	Total	**7**	**6**	**13**	**4**	**10**	**14**

Source: GAO analysis of FSM single audit reports.

Notes: In the FSM, we focused our review on the National Government and the state governments of Chuuk and Pohnpei. We did not include in our review the state governments of Yap and Kosrae. See app. I for additional discussion of scope.

[a]Data do not include findings for the component units of the FSM National Government, such as the College of Micronesia.

Table 17: Number of Material Weaknesses and Significant Deficiencies Reported in Single Audit Reports for the Republic of the Marshall Islands (RMI), Fiscal Years 2006 through 2011

	Reportable findings on internal control over financial reporting			Reportable findings on internal control over compliance with federal awards		
	Material weaknesses	Significant deficiencies	Total	Material weaknesses	Significant deficiencies	Total
2006	1	0	1	4	6	10
2007	3	0	3	3	5	8
2008	2	0	2	3	4	7
2009	5	0	5	8	3	11
2010	8	0	8	7	0	7
2011	11	0	11	8	0	8

Source: GAO analysis of RMI single audit reports.

Note: Data do not include findings for the component units of the RMI government, such as the College of the Marshall Islands.

Internal Control over Financial Reporting

The single audit reports for fiscal year 2011, the most recent year for which reports were available during our review, identified a combined total of 13 material weaknesses and significant deficiencies which relate to the FSM's fiscal year 2011 financial statements, and a total of 11 for the RMI's statements (see tables 16 and 17, respectively). These findings indicated a lack of effective internal controls over collection of travel advances and the lack of ability to adequately safeguard assets; to ensure that transactions are properly recorded; and to prevent or detect fraud, waste, and abuse. For example, the material weaknesses reported in FSM's fiscal year 2011 single audit report included (1) the lack of timely reconciliation of the Holding Bank Account,[9] (2) the lack of adequate monitoring of collection of travel advances, (3) the lack of timely and accurate reconciliation of general ledger accounts, and (4) the lack of adequate reconciliation of and accounting for fixed assets.[10] In RMI's fiscal year 2011 single audit report, the auditors found material weaknesses that included (1) the lack of documentation to determine whether certain costs were allowable, (2) lack of inventory of fixed assets,

---

[9]Compact sector grant drawdowns and deposits are made to the holding bank account.

[10]The FSM National Government's 2011 Single Audit report in Note 1 (M) of the Notes to the Financial Statements reports that fixed assets or capital assets include, but are not limited to, computer equipment, furniture, equipment, machinery and motor vehicles.

(3) lack of general ledger account reconciliation, and (4) lack of internal controls over bank wire transfers.

We found that 6 of the 7 material weaknesses in internal control over financial reporting contained in the FSM's fiscal year 2011 single audit report were recurring problems from the previous year or had been reported for several years. Below are two examples:

- General ledger account reconciliations were not performed in a timely manner or accurately. The lack of timely and accurate account reconciliations may affect accurate reporting and timely submission of the single audit report.

- Fixed-asset records were not periodically reconciled and timely recorded. Likewise, 8 of the 11 material weakness findings in the RMI's fiscal year 2011 single audit report were recurring problems from the previous year or had been reported for several years, including these examples:

- Fixed assets records were not being periodically reconciled and recorded in a timely manner.

- Procurement requirements were not followed, such as the lack of the required three price quotations for an expenditure.

The FSM and RMI have developed corrective action plans to address financial statement findings in the 2011 single audit.[11]

Compliance with Requirements of Federal Awards

In addition to the auditor's report on financial statement findings, FSM and RMI auditors issuing an entity's single audit reports also issue an opinion on the entity's compliance with requirements of major federal programs. Of the 24 single audit reports submitted by the FSM national and state governments and the RMI for fiscal years 2006 through 2011, 19 received qualified opinions regarding compliance with requirements of major federal programs. The remaining six received unqualified opinions; Pohnpei received 4 of the 6 unqualified opinions.

---

[11]Office of Management and Budget (OMB) Circular A-133, "Audits of States, Local Governments, and Non-Profit Organizations," requires the auditee to communicate what actions will be taken to address the audit finding.

In the 2011 single audit reports on compliance with requirements of major federal programs, auditors reported 14 material weaknesses and significant deficiencies for the FSM and 8 for the RMI (see tables 16 and 17, respectively). For example, in the FSM, the reported material weaknesses included (1) the lack of internal controls over compliance with cash management requirements, (2) lack of funds control to prevent disbursements in excess of available funds, and (3) lack of controls over property accountability. In the RMI, findings that were material weaknesses included (1) a lack of fixed assets inventory control, (2) the lack of internal controls over compliance with cash management requirements, (3) the lack of internal controls over procurement, and (4) the lack of adequate documentation of cost allowability.

We found that 13 of the 14 findings from the 2011 FSM and state governments' single audit reports, and 7 of the 8 findings from the 2011 RMI single audit report, were recurring problems from the previous year or had recurred for several years.[12] In contrast, for the FSM only 5 of the 41 findings from the 2005 single audit reports and, for the RMI, only 5 of the 13 findings from the 2005 single audit report were recurring problems from the previous year or had recurred for several years. The FSM and RMI 2011 single audit reports stated that the FSM and RMI have developed corrective action plans to address all the 2011 single audit reports' findings on compliance with requirements of major federal programs.

As the count of single audit findings in table 17 demonstrate, material weaknesses related to internal controls have increased over the last 3 years. As we have previously reported, weaknesses in internal controls may lead to fraud, waste, and abuse.[13] Since late 2010, 22 cases involving collusion among three employees of the RMI Ministry of Finance, three employees of the RMI Ministry of Health, and three local businesses are being prosecuted in the RMI. These 22 cases involve a total of approximately $550,000 in compact funding. According to an OIA

---

[12]In October 2003, GAO reported that "The percentage of each auditee's single audit findings that recurred 3 or more years over the 5-year period of our review ranged from RMI's high of 69 percent to a low of 17 percent for the FSM." See GAO, *Compacts of Free Association: Single Audits Demonstrate Accountability Problems over Compact Funds*, GAO-04-7 (Washington, D.C.: Oct. 7, 2003).

[13]GAO, *Education Financial Management: Weak Internal Controls Led to Instances of Fraud and Other Improper Payments*, GAO-02-406 (Washington, D.C.: Mar. 28, 2002).

official, this fraud was not uncovered through an audit; rather, it was detected when the leader of the group of government workers involved in the fraud tried to pick up a vendor payment from the RMI Ministry of Finance, raising suspicions and leading to an investigation. According to an OIA official, in 2012, two former RMI government workers were charged with 25 counts of theft related to 20 checks from the government valued at $350,000. They received fines and 5-year prison sentences. According to an RMI official, the investigation is ongoing, and the RMI Office of the Auditor General (OAG) has collaborated with the RMI Attorney General since the start of the investigation. Furthermore, the OAG has taken its own action to better detect fraud by creating a new investigation unit within the OAG to conduct investigations of suspected fraudulent activities and created a confidential fraud hotline where RMI citizens can contact the OAG to report instances of fraud, waste, and abuse for further investigation.

According to an RMI official, over the past 5 years, the RMI Auditor General has focused on financial and compliance audits, including the single audits of RMI government agencies. The OAG also conducted its own audits of component units for fiscal years 2006 through 2011. According to the RMI Auditor General, because of insufficient staff, the OAG performed only 1 performance audit over the past several years,[14] and additional staff would be needed to enable the office to address the demand for fraud investigations. Recognizing the magnitude of potential fraud, OIA authorized a Technical Assistance grant of $110,500 in 2012 to recruit a Certified Fraud Examiner for RMI. According to a RMI OAG official, as of June 2013, the RMI had not filled this position.

[14]Performance audits are defined as audits that provide findings or conclusions based on an evaluation of sufficient, appropriate evidence against criteria. Performance audits provide objective analysis to assist management and those charged with governance and oversight in using the information to improve program performance and operations, reduce costs, facilitate decision making by parties with responsibility to oversee or initiate corrective action, and contribute to public accountability. GAO previously reported on the lack of performance audits of compact sector grants. See GAO, *Compacts of Free Association: Micronesia and the Marshall Islands Face Challenges in Planning for Sustainability, Measuring Progress, and Ensuring Accountability*, GAO-07-163 (Washington, D.C.: Dec. 15, 2006), p. 43.

Appendix VIII: Office of Insular Affairs (OIA) Staffing Projections for Compact Oversight, Fiscal Years 2010–2013

Position	Location	Projected need				Actual supply				Shortages (as of 2013)
		2010	2011	2012	2013	2010	2011	2012	2013	
Lead Program Grants Specialist	Honolulu, HI	1	1	1	1	1	1	1	1	0
Education Grants Specialist	Honolulu, HI	1	2	2	2	1	1	1	1	1
Health Grants Specialist	Honolulu, HI	1	1	1	1	1	1	1	1	0
Fiscal Program Specialist	Honolulu, HI	1	4	4	4	1	1	1	1	3
Grants Specialist	Federated States of Micronesia	1	1	1	1	0	0	0	1	0
Insular Policy Specialist	Federated States of Micronesia	1	1	1	1	0	0	0	0	1
Grants Specialist	Republic of the Marshall Islands	1	1	1	1	1	1	1	1	0
Totals		**7**	**11**	**11**	**11**	**5**	**5**	**5**	**6**	**5**

Source: GAO analysis of OIA data.

Note: Data are from the Department of the Interior's OIA 2010 workforce plan and interviews with OIA officials.

Appendix IX: Comments from the U.S. Department of the Interior

 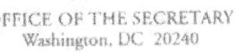 

United States Department of the Interior

OFFICE OF THE SECRETARY
Washington, DC 20240

TAKE PRIDE
IN AMERICA

AUG - 7 2013

Mr. David Gootnick
Director, International Affairs and Trade
U.S. Government Accountability Office
Washington, D.C. 20548

Dear Mr. Gootnick:

Thank you for the opportunity to respond to the U.S. Government Accountability Office (GAO) draft report, entitled, "COMPACTS OF FREE ASSOCIATION: Micronesia and the Marshall Islands Continue to Face Challenges Measuring Progress and Ensuring Accountability" (Report).

The Report fairly summarizes activities and results of Compact of Free Association (COFA) financial assistance used in the Federated States of Micronesia (FSM) and the Republic of the Marshall Islands (RMI) in fiscal years (FY) 2007 through 2011. The Report identifies issues related to data reliability in reporting program outcomes in the health and education sectors, difficulties in providing for sustainable services as COFA grants decline, continuing problems with accountability and the difficulties of the three governments in providing oversight of COFA programs. The Report also notes that the Department of the Interior and other U.S. agencies through the Joint Economic Management Committee (JEMCO) and the Joint Economic Management and Financial Accountability Committee (JEMFAC) have continually pushed for improvement in these areas by the FSM and RMI.

The Report recommends that the Secretary of the Interior take five actions to address the identified shortfalls. The Department of the Interior agrees generally with these recommendations for action and discusses each below.

- *Direct the Assistant Secretary of Insular Affairs, as Chairman of JEMCO, to coordinate with other JEMCO member U.S. agencies to have JEMCO take all necessary steps, or as the administrator of compact grants to directly take the necessary steps, to ensure that the FSM (1) completes satisfactory plans to address annual decrements in compact funds, (2) produces reliable indicator data used to track progress in education and health, and (3) addresses all single audit findings in a timely manner.*

The Department and U.S. members of JEMCO are currently taking steps to address decrement planning and to improve performance. All FSM states have completed decrement plans that are satisfactory. JEMCO has requested the FSM national government to detail its plan at the August 21, 2013, meeting.

We will continue to work with the FSM to increase the reliability of its data, noting the difficulty of reconciling five different state and national government reporting systems. This issue will be discussed at the upcoming JEMCO meeting. The Department will take actions necessary to address audit findings in a timely manner and in accordance with applicable Federal regulations. It must be noted, however, that although OIA, in its role as Cognizant Agency for Audits, has responsibilities for monitoring the resolution of specific findings, other single audit findings may only be resolved by the Federal grantor agency.

- *Direct the Assistant Secretary of Insular Affairs, as Chairman of JEMFAC, to coordinate with other JEMFAC member U.S. agencies to have JEMFAC take all necessary steps, or as the administrator of compact grants to directly take all necessary steps, to ensure that the RMI (1) completes satisfactory plans to address annual decrements in compact funds, (2) produces reliable indicator data used to track progress in education and health, and (3) addresses all single audit findings in a timely manner.*

As with the similar recommendation related to JEMCO and the FSM, the Department and other U.S. JEMFAC members have worked with the RMI to make improvements in all three areas. As noted in the Report, the U.S. JEMFAC members notified the RMI in April 2013 that the United States was considering withholding FY 2014 funding if an adequate decrement plan and budget framework is not presented to the JEMFAC at its August 2013 meeting. Additionally, the Office of Insular Affairs (OIA) Accountability Specialist has visited the RMI, most recently in July 2013, to continue assistance that includes resolving single audit findings. OIA has also withheld reallocation of prior year compact funding balances until the RMI is current with single audits and questioned cost resolution.

The Report makes two identical recommendations regarding accountability:

- *Consult with other grantor agencies to determine whether the FSM national government or any FSM states meet the criteria to be designated as a high-risk grant recipient for noncompact funds, or whether other steps should be taken to improve accountability.*

- *Consult with other grantor agencies to determine whether the RMI meets the criteria to be designated as a high-risk recipient for noncompact funds, or whether other steps should be taken to improve accountability.*

Although we are unaware of any Federal interagency practice to jointly designate a grantee as high risk, the Department will discuss the GAO recommendation as part of OIA's ongoing communications with other Federal agencies, both directly and through the RIX's Federal Regional Council and its Outer Pacific Committee. OIA notes that, as part of the annual single audit process, independent auditors identify whether the auditee may be considered a low-risk auditee, and the respective single audit reports made available to all Federal agencies have identified consistently that the RMI Government, FSM National Government, Chuuk State Government, FSM, and Yap State Government, FSM, are not low-risk auditees. The Department understands that all "high risk" designations are grantor agency decisions based on specific circumstances found in a grant program. The Department cannot direct other agencies to take action with regard to individual grant issues, including resolution of questioned costs and other grant-specific issues.

The final recommendation of the Report addresses staffing issues at the Department of the Interior:

- *Take actions to correct the disproportionate staffing shortage related to compact grant implementation and oversight.*

The Department acknowledges that additional staffing would result in increased oversight of COFA activities. Unfortunately, until an annual budget reflecting the President's priorities is enacted, it is unlikely that all the necessary positions can be filled. OIA has considered requesting special permission to fill another Education Specialist position, but has decided to await notification of FY 2014 funding levels before taking action. Any other increases in oversight personnel will be requested and approved through the annual budget process.

Thank you for the opportunity to comment.

Sincerely,

Thomas Bussanich

Nikolao I. Pula
Director
Office of Insular Affairs

Appendix X: Comments from the Federated States of Micronesia National Government

EMBASSY OF THE
FEDERATED STATES OF MICRONESIA
1725 N St. NW
Washington, DC 20036

Tel: 202-223-4383 Toll Free: 1-877-730-9753 Fax: 202-223-4391

Emails: admin@fsmembassydc.org
         fsmdc1@gmail.com
Website: www.fsmembassydc.org

August 30, 2013

David B Gootnick, PhD
Director
International Affairs & Trade
US Government Accountability Office
441 G Street NW
Washington, DC   20548

Dear Dr. Gootnick:

On behalf of the FSM Government, we wish to thank the US Congress and the GAO for the continued support and commitment of resources to the FSM. We also appreciate the opportunity to provide our comments on the subject report. The report highlights GAO's findings on three issues, namely: (1) need to plan for the annual decrement in compact funding; (2) data reliability issues for health and education indicators; and (3) financial accountability over use of Compact and US Federal Program grants. We agree on the importance of these three issues to the successful implementation of the Amended Compact and offer the following general observations and comments on findings and recommendations offered in the report.

Annual Decrement Management Plans

The FSM Government welcomes GAO's observations on the need for finalizing plans for managing the annual decrements in compact funding. As recognized in the report, the FSM States have completed difficult exercises in identifying cuts in their recurrent budgets in anticipation of the scheduled reductions in compact funding each year as well as the expected decline in the real value of the compact grants due to the partial inflation indexation of these grants. The States planning exercise has gone beyond simply creating room for the expected cuts in compact funding to also creating room for the expected reduction in real value of grants. As pointed out in the report, these identified budget reductions are to take effect in FY2014, 2017, and 2020. The FY2014 budget reductions will be sufficient to address annual decrements expected in FY2014, 2015, and 2016. While the focus of the State Plans is on expenditure reductions, revenue-enhancing we're also endorsed to be pursued aggressively by the States Governments in order to alleviate the need to undertake the budget cuts identified for FY2017 and 2020.

Sector budgets account for less than 20% of the National Government budget. Over the past two fiscal years, JEMCO has made certain decisions that have substantially reduced the use of sector grants for recurrent government budgets in the national government. Recurrent government budgets have been replaced with specific JEMCO supported projects

1

in health and education such as 100% coverage of NMCT testing, School Accreditation Program, Teacher Certification, Specialized Medical Team, NCD funding, etc. As documented in our July 1st, 2013 letter to US members on JEMCO, these measures combined with the State Plans addressing the annual decrement should suffice in meeting the narrower requirements on the annual decrement management plan.

The broader planning issues outlined in the JEMCO resolution calling for the Long-Term Fiscal Framework goes beyond calling for annual decrement management plans. The broader planning objectives called for in JEMCO Resolution 2010-2 are being addressed by the FSM Government in the context of the 2023 Planning Committee's work initiated by the FSM President. One of the primary objectives of the 2023 Planning Committee is to identify ways to intensify private sector growth as part of our solution to the scheduled reductions in compact funding.

On the issue of resource sharing between the National and States Governments, the FSM leadership is working together very closely to arrive at a decision that will be beneficial to both levels of government and at the same time facilitate greater effectiveness in meeting the development objectives of the FSM.

Data Reliability:

The report also points out JEMCO's concerns about the reliability of FSM's health and education indicators inhibiting our ability to determine progress in these two sectors. The report also found that the FSM has yet to comply with the JEMCO requirement to obtain an independent assessment and verification of health and education indicator data. As reported at the JEMCO Annual Meeting last week, the FSM National Department of Education has already contracted Mid-continent Research for Education and Learning (McREL) to conduct the independent verification of performance indicators and quality data for the education indicators. This week, August 26-30, 2013, the McREL Team is in FSM carrying out the first phase of the work. The scope of services includes the following:

- Conduct an assessment of the appropriateness of the nation's education data framework;
- Verify the soundness of process used, whether manual or computerized;
- Validate the reliability of inputs to documentation; and
- Ensure the verifiability of data at both points of entry and in abstracted reports.

On the health indicator data, the FSM Government through its FSM Department of Health and Social Affairs issued a request for proposal, after consulting with OIA, following its standard bidding procedure. Only one proposal was received from outside the FSM. However, the company requested an amount much higher than the amount approved by OIA for this activity. After a series of negotiation, the company declined to carry out the work. As a result, the FSM Department of Health and Social Affairs had initiated a project to

2

clean and automate where automation is feasible; its health information databases and institute a web-based reporting system for the 14 health indicators.

Financial Accountability

Our goal has been and remains to obtain unqualified opinions on both financial and compliance. As noted in the report, the FSM National and States Governments have come a long way since 2006 but we recognize that there is still room for improvement. In the recent FY2012 Audit, for the National Government the total number of findings on internal control over financial reporting total three, and findings on internal control over compliance with federal awards was nine, a decrease from fiscal year 2011.

In previous years, we focused largely on resolving the qualifications on the FSM National Governments financial statements, which resulted in the unqualified opinion on its financials. With the resolution of all the qualifications, our objective now is to maintain the unqualified opinion on the financials and at the same time reduce the number of findings by twenty percent each fiscal year by doing the following:

1. Staff Development to: (a) Understand and enforce all applicable federal regulations, (b) Continue to provide hands on training on daily operations, and (c) Improve understanding of accounting principles;
2. Improve processes to ensure government expenditures are appropriately supported and filed;
3. Monthly reconciliations of General Ledger Accounts;
4. Monitoring of government fixed assets; and
5. Establishing a cash management/Fixed Assets Maintenance Plan.

With the Assistance of USDA Graduate School, we have developed finance performance measures to gauge performance. Among these performance measures is the monitoring of Outstanding Travel Advances, which continues to be a repeat finding on the FSM National Governments audit. Additional measures have been put in place to encourage timely filing of travel vouchers. Additionally, as part of our efforts in resolving the cash management citations for the Airport Improvement Projects, the Department has submitted to the Federal Aviation Authority a request for an average clearance pattern and is still awaiting a response.

We will continue working together with all the departments, offices and agencies to minimize and eventually eliminate remaining findings so as to achieve unqualified audit opinion on both financial and compliance at both National and States levels.

Having indicated the above, we wish to register that we are surprised by the heavy emphasis on the possibility of achieving increased accountability over non-Compact grant funds through a "high-risk" designation. We are assured however by the knowledge that the process involved in a "high-risk" designation is not an arbitrary one.

3

As we have observed in the past, we believe that much insight into the compact implementation challenges and successes can be gained by a mere separation of the reporting on the FSM and RMI.

Once again, we reiterate our appreciation for the opportunity to present our comments on the draft report.

Respectfully submitted,

Asterio Takesy
FSM Ambassador to the United States

4

Appendix XI: Comments from the Government of the Republic of the Marshall Islands

Note: GAO comments in response to this letter, supplementing those in the report text, appear at the end of this appendix.

EMBASSY OF THE REPUBLIC OF THE MARSHALL ISLANDS
2433 Massachusetts Avenue, N.W.,
Washington, D.C. 20008
Tel. # (202) 234-5414 * Fax # (202) 232-3236 * E-mail: info@rmiembassyus.org

September 5, 2013

Mr. Emil E Friberg, Jr.
Assistant Director/Senior Economist at GAO
Washington, DC

Dear Mr. Friberg,

The Embassy of the Republic of the Marshall Islands has the honor to forward the attached comments by the RMI Government to the draft GAO report entitled, *"Micronesia and the Marshall Islands Continue to Face Challenges Measuring Progress and Ensuring Accountability"*, GAO report number, *"GAO-13-675"*.

Sincerely,

H.E. Mr. Charles Paul
Ambassador of the Republic of the Marshall Islands to the United States of America

cc: Hon. Mr. Phillip Muller, Minister of Foreign Affairs, Republic of the Marshall Islands
        Kino S. Kabua, Secretary of Foreign Affairs

Page numbers in draft report mentioned in the letter may differ from those in this report.

RESPONSE AND COMMENTS OF THE GOVERNMENT OF THE REPUBLIC OF THE MARSHALL ISLANDS TO THE U.S. GOVERNMENT ACCOUNTABILITY OFFICE REPORT "COMPACTS OF FREE ASSOCIATION, MICRONEISA AND MARSHALL ISLANDS CONTINUE TO FACE CHALLENGES MEASURING PROGRESS AND ENSURING ACCOUNTABILITY"

The Government of the Republic of the Marshall Islands (GRMI) wishes to convey its appreciation to the United States Government Accountability Office (GAO) for extending the deadline for commenting to its DRAFT Report. GRMI's comments are stated below.

TECHNICAL COMMENTS

Ministry of Finance (MOF)

1. Single Audit (Cover Page and Pages 38-40)

See comment 1.

   a. As noted in the GAO report, GRMI's unresolved prior year questioned costs totaled $7.4 million at the end of fiscal year 2011. Before the commencement of the fiscal year 2012 audit, the Secretary of Finance took several steps to better manage the audit fieldwork process and reduce prior year questioned costs. These measures included greater supervisory oversight and follow-through on missing procurement documentation and preliminary questioned cost citations. As a result, GRMI was able to reduce its questioned costs in the fiscal year 2012 compliance report to a record low of $35,000. Similarly, MOF staff began a detailed examination of all prior year audit findings and worked closely with the Department of the Interior (DOI) audit resolution official to obtain the necessary documentation to clear these questioned costs. Although this official's reinstatement letter has not been received as of the date of these comments, the Secretary of Finance is now confident there will be timely resolution of all prior year questioned costs.

   b. MOF believes that internal controls are now in place to detect and deter fraud, waste or non-compliance with the *Fiscal Procedures Agreement* (FPA) or other U.S. Federal regulations. As such, it does not believe that any special conditions or restrictions for unsatisfactory performance or failure to comply with grant terms are warranted. Moreover, MOF does not believe that an Office of Insular Affairs (OIA) "intervention" is necessary or desirable for improving financial accountability over Compact or other U.S. Federal grants. Although there will always be areas in grant management that require special focus, MOF has actively solicited other third-party support for its reforms. In both fiscal years 2012 and 2013, MOF had increased access to financial assistance from the Asian

1

See comment 2.

Development Bank, World Bank and International Monetary Fund. Noting the decrement affecting Compact sector resources and recurring OIA staffing shortages to assist with greater financial accountability, the GRMI believes that utilizing these other third parties is the preferred option for better public management of its public finances.

2. MTBIF (Pages 19 and 20) and Compact Grant Decrements (Cover Page, Pages 12, and 46)

   a. GRMI submitted plans that w*ill address the decrements* during the Mid-Year Joint Economic Management and Financial Accountability Committee (JEMFAC) meeting in March 2011 and prior to the Annual JEMFAC meeting in August 2013, entitled: *"Decrement Strategy & MTBIF Policy Framework Paper, FY11-14"* and *"Medium Term Budget and Investment Framework (MTBIF), Compact Sector Report"*, respectively. Both plans outlined initiatives that will address the decrements in Compact funding.

   b. GRMI will address its long-term fiscal planning initiatives as part of an expanded narrative of its MTBIF submission. The GRMI has submitted its 2014 MTBIF and *Fiscal Management Model* to OIA prior to the Annual JEMFAC meeting in August 2013 and believes these documents address the concerns expressed by U.S. officials at various times as well as embed expenditure and revenue assumptions as a result of the decrement in compact sector funding through fiscal year 2023. It will continue to revise the MTBIF framework each year or at suitable intervals as required for clarifications or by changes in circumstances and further add such narrative addendums to address major decrement issues whenever required. MOF believes, however, that this document is useful as a policy guide and planning tool, not as a basis for micro-managing line-item adjustments in particular sub-accounts.

   c. While acknowledging the efficacy of a MTBIF and related decrement study as a planning tool, the GRMI is concerned about certain scope elements included in the proposed JEMFAC resolution 2010-1: *Long-Term Fiscal Planning* that are no longer accurate. First of all, as indicated in successive single audit reports, there is no long-term "unsustainable growth in government wage bills," and revenues are increasing significantly in many areas. Secondly, tax reform initiatives are on schedule and have broad-based political support. Moreover, commenting on subjective interpretations such as "apparent political obstacles" in any fiscal plan does not move the discussion further along with respect to more efficient tax administration, increasing revenues or management of US grants. Finally,

2

economic activity is neither stagnant nor declining as evidenced in a recent report contracted by OIA. Noting these changed scope items from the original resolution, MOF believes the usefulness of a decrement plan is as a policy guide and planning tool – not as a basis for imposing line-item expenditure ceilings which seldom reflect broader policy goals.

Ministry of Health (MOH)

3. MOH data (Pages 20, 33, and footnote 45)

    a. ˏMOH acknowledges the GAO's report and wish to provide the following feedback for further clarification on some of the points expressed. Furthermore, MOH agrees with the comments expressed on MOH's data reliability. As stated, reliability question stems from late entries and having multiple international databases.

    b. Currently, there are 52 health centers spread throughout the 29 atolls and receiving the data on time is always a challenge. In addition, MOH lacks proper personnel to concentrate solely on data encoding. Health officers and/or nurses are also responsible for data encoding in addition to their regular duties of providing health services. In an effort to remedy this, MOH has requested and received support from some of the Federal Grants namely the Prevention & Public Health Fund to support for additional data entry personnel.

    c. MOH wishes to further clarify GAO's reference to the leprosy data as having no basis for judgment. Prior to FY2011, there was only 1 public Health nurse responsible for Leprosy who also had other responsibilities in other Public Health Programs. FY2011 was the first year MOH established the Leprosy Program and dedicated 5 staff solely for said Program. In MOH's view, the high detection rate over the past 2 years is a result of having the Program and the necessary personnel in place.

    d. In FY2011, MOH did receive assistance from United Nations Development Program (UNDP) to aid with the Health Information management improvement initiative. However, the UN Volunteer left prior to the contract or any of the assessments were completed. Following the UN Volunteer's departure, MOH resubmitted its request to UNDP for further assistance. Selections were made, however, the candidates declined later on.

    e. In April of 2013, MOH worked with the Pacific Islands Health Officer's Association (PIHOA) requesting for assistance with its data assessment but also

3

included, as part of the request, review of the reporting framework. Currently, PIHOA is awaiting MOH's request to be officially submitted. It is important to note that MOH intends to submit said proposal to PIHOA to review and update RMI's core performance indicators (CPIs) to assure that they are still relevant and institute performance management processes for CPIs.

Ministry of Education (MOE)

4. MOE indicators

a. *Page 26 - "The RMI established 20 indicators to track progress in education..."* We believe the United States, specifically OIA, put forward these 20 indicators. The level of consultation with GRMI was not sufficient to establish adequate level of ownership of indicators. GRMI has been reporting on these indicators since the inception of the amended Compact. Some of the indicators are not useful anymore and should be deleted from the list while more useful indicators might need to be added. Moving forward, it is recommended that two sides revisit these set of indicators.

b. *Page 27 - ..."data for 4 (indicators) could not be used...because of reliability problems..."* We agree that data for the rest of the indicators are not 100% accurate; but we think they are the best we can provide given the large number of small schools spread out over a large ocean area, and the deficient state of our transportation and communication system (for example, no internet access on almost all outer islands.)

c. *Page 27 - "Dropout rate....lack of outer island data; missing data"* The RMI population, especially in the outer islands, is highly mobile in any given year, moving not only from island to island within an atoll, but also from outer islands to outer islands and to Majuro and Ebeye and back to home island, and even to the U.S. We provided the data we can in this area with the idea that they are approximate indicators.

d. *Page 28 - "...in fiscal years 2007 and 2008 RMI used the Pacific Island Literacy Test...whereas in 2009 it began using the Marshall Islands Standardized Test, so year-to year changes in the data for this indicator are not reliable..."* Development and implementation of the Marshall Islands Standardized Test (MISAT) series was undertaken given that the Pacific Island Literacy (PIL) Test was discontinued by its regional provider.

4

See comment 3.

See comment 4.

e. *Page 48 – "However, because of data reliability issues, neither country can demonstrate whether they have made progress toward their goals in these sectors."* Making positive gains in student performance take time. Improvements have been made and are noted in teacher quality, student performance and facilities improvements. The report itself alluded to these improvements. The standards applied for evaluating progress are not self-evident and so a general statement such as the above is questionable at best.

5. Supplemental Education Grant (SEG)

a. Regarding Page 7, it is important to note that the SEG is one year behind (i.e. while Compact base grants are for Fiscal Year 2014, SEG for fiscal year 2013 is provided in fiscal year 2014). Moreover, the amount of $6.1 million stated in the amended Compact has not been provided to the RMI. In fact, the SEG has been declining since 2005 from $6.1 to $5.5 in 2013 and has never included inflation amounts. The SEG allocation for RMI in 2013 was adversely affected by the U.S. Government sequestration.

b. In footnote # 17, although the amended Compact provides that the SEG "shall be used and monitored in accordance to an agreement" between DOI, Department of Education (DOE), Department of Health and Human Services (HHS) and the Department of Labor (DOL), the RMI has not received a copy despite repeated requests at JEMFAC meetings.

See comment 5.

c. In order to be comprehensive on the use of the SEG, the GRMI feels that the direct quote from the FPA in Page 7 should be expanded to include "Funds may also be used to provide aid to students at post-secondary institutions based on financial need, and to design and develop innovative and strategic programs or activities that enable the education system to provide improved direct educational services and meet performance accountability requirements. Funds awarded under the Supplemental Education Grant shall not be used for school construction or remodeling; general operational costs (other than general operational costs of programs and activities funded by the Supplemental Educational Grant); or teacher salaries, except for the salaries of teachers, teaching assistants, paraprofessionals, or instructors who are needed to carry out programs or activities supported by the Supplemental Education Grant. Funds awarded under the Supplemental Education Grant are not to be taken into account when satisfying the priority to be given to education and health when awarding Sector Grants…"

5

Public Management Unit (PMU)

6. On-site Visits

See comment 6.

    a. *Page 28: "Many of the safety doors that we observed at our selected schools were either off their hinges and moved to one side or propped open with an object. Officials told us that this problem occurred because the doors had not been properly installed."* At Rairok Elementary School (RRES), the problem fitting the door to the wall has been corrected by the Contractor as the hinges were not properly installed at the time of inspection by GAO. We observed too that these safety doors, mostly on 2-storey buildings are designed & built with special framing, aluminum hinges & locks because of its weight and size. If not well taken cared by end-user on proper usage, it is really prone to damage. In some instances, kids are seen playing with these doors and damages are reported happening at Delap Elementary School (DES), Rita Elementary School (RES) and Laura Elementary School (LES) where MOE Maintenance Crew started the repairs. Outer island schools do not have this kind of doors. PMU will check with the Designer (BECA) to provide alternative replacement door using stainless steel hinges in lieu of the aluminum hinges and increase the number of hinges installed per door.

See comment 7.

    b. *Page 28: "However, we did find that several of the water tanks at the school were not connected to any of the buildings."* MOE is currently fixing the catchment tanks apparently damaged by students. Intentionally disconnected by MOE Maintenance Crew for repair purposes. It is worthwhile to note that plastic catchment tanks are easily vandalized even with fencing as in the case of RES where the chain link fence is cut open by outsiders to draw water from the tanks. The issue of these damages are due to unsecured campuses (no fencing and security), which could easily be vandalized by outsiders.

See comment 8.

    c. *Page 28: "At another school that we visited, Laura Elementary school, classrooms in the new building had desks, chairs, and electricity, but an old building that was still used lacked electricity."* All classrooms in LES are hooked up to power (Majuro Energy Company) and MOE Maintenance does not recall any complaints of lack of power. It might be due to some internal electrical problem occurring at the time.

See comment 9.

    d. *Page 28: "At Delap Elementary, the classrooms had electricity, we were informed, but running water was available only twice weekly, which meant that the school had to rely on a rainwater catchment facility for some of its needs."* DES is provided with 4-1500 gallons catchment for most of its needs but is also connected to the city water thru a by-pass valve, in case run-off is low. Majuro Water and Sewer Company (MWSC) rations water during dryer months where catchment tanks are also low or have no water. MOE at one time replaced the damaged pump but currently DES has no problem with water.

6

See comment 10.

e. *Page 28-29: "On Ebeye, we visited a school in Gugeegue that had consistent electricity, we were told. We observed the chairs, desks, and textbooks on our visit. However, we were also shown one of the school buildings being used for classroom that was considered unsafe."* In one of our inspection in Ebeye dated November 2011, PMU had issued a notice to Kwajalein Atoll High School (KAHS) and MOE that for safety reasons, the old building at KAHS had to be abandoned. During the time of the GAO visit (2013), MOE & KAHS started constructing a 3-classroom building to replace the unsafe structure. With the concurrence of DOI, PMU had processed a purchase requisition to purchase construction materials while MOE & KAHS agreed to provide the labor component. To date, the old building has been abandoned and KAHS is reportedly occupying the new 3-classroom building.

Office of Compact Implementation (OCI)

7. Typos

a. In footnote # 36, instead of "JEMCO", it should be "JEMFAC". RMI did not just make verbal commitments but also in writing explaining the factors that would affect the development of a decrement plan which was provided on March 2013.

b. In footnote # 72, instead of ".7", it should be "7".

c. In Page 43, instead of "foreign policy officer", it should be "foreign service officer".

d. Also in Page 43, instead of "RMI Chief Secretary", it should be the "Office of the Chief Secretary".

e. In footnote # 90, instead of "Ministry of Finance", it should be the "Ministry of Foreign Affairs".

8. Clarification

See comment 11.

a. In Page 43, RMI officials meant that the Office of the Chief Secretary did not have the authority to withhold funds but if it had the authority to do so, it would be the last resort. This comment is in relation to submissions of quarterly reports from the Compact Ministries and Agencies. Said submissions are to be provided to Office of Compact Implementation (OCI) through the Office of the Chief Secretary in order to receive these reports in a timely manner.

7

ADDITIONAL COMMENTS

<u>Five-Year Review</u>

1. There has been no action on the First Five-Year Review report despite recommendations from the GRMI to improve the implementation of the Compact, as amended. U.S. Government has not initiated the Second Five-Year Review although the amended Compact is now in its 10th year.

<u>Trust Fund</u>

See comment 12.

2. In Page 1 of the report, GRMI feels that reference to the intent of the RMI Trust Fund to provide an annual source of revenue post-2023 should cite GAO's *Compacts of Free Association: Trust Funds for Micronesia and the Marshall Islands May Not Provide Sustainable Income. GAO-07-513, Washington, D.C.: June 15, 2007.*

<u>Recommendations by GAO</u>

3. With respect to the recommendations to JEMFAC in Page 48, JEMFAC has recently passed the JEMFAC Resolution 2013-1 to use carry-over funds to address one or more of the following three areas: to assist the GRMI to complete satisfactory plans to address annual decrements in Compact funds; to produce reliable indicator data used to track progress in education and health; and/or to address all single audit findings in a timely manner.

8

The following are GAO's comments on the letter from the government of
the Republic of the Marshall Islands (RMI) dated September 5, 2013. We
comment only to note where we addressed an RMI comment by adding
or updating information in the report, or to note areas of concern.

GAO Comments

1. In its comments, the RMI stated that the RMI Minister of Finance took
   steps to better manage the audit fieldwork process and reduced the
   2012 questioned costs to approximately $35,000 and also began a
   detailed examination of all prior year questioned costs. We added this
   information in footnote 81 on page 44.

2. The RMI noted in its comments that it had provided the U.S.–RMI
   Joint Economic Management and Financial Accountability Committee
   (JEMFAC) with updated plans, as required, prior to the August 2013
   JEMFAC meeting. We updated our report to reflect that the RMI
   submitted an updated medium-term budget and investment
   framework dated August 2013 along with several budget portfolio
   statements for fiscal year 2014, including statements for the
   departments of health and education. On the basis of information we
   received at the August 2013 JEMFAC meeting, we further noted that
   the RMI government considers this to be its decrement plan, but also
   that the information was provided to the U.S. members of the
   JEMFAC 3 days prior to the annual meeting, and according to these
   members, they did not have sufficient time to review it and determine
   whether or not it meets the requirements of the JEMFAC resolution.
   We added this updated information on page 23 of the report.

3. In its comments, the RMI stated that it believes the United States,
   specifically the Office of Insular Affairs (OIA), put forward the RMI's 20
   education indicators and that the level of consultation with the RMI
   government was not sufficient to establish adequate level of
   ownership of the indicators. At the August 2013 JEMFAC meeting, the
   Chairman of JEMFAC stated that the 20 education indicators were
   developed collaboratively between the U.S. and the RMI. At the same
   meeting, the Education Grant Manager of the Office of Insular Affairs
   confirmed this point.

4. The RMI noted in its comments that improvements have been made
   in teacher quality, student performance, and facilities, which, they
   stated, the report itself alludes to. The RMI noted that making positive
   gains in student performance takes time. The standards for evaluating
   progress are the RMI's 20 education indicators, which it has tracked
   since 2005 in response to a JEMFAC resolution, as noted in the

report. However, in order to use the indicators to assess progress for the compacts as a whole, we first needed to determine if the data supporting the indicators were reliable. As our report states, two out of the subset of five education indicators we examined were deemed sufficiently reliable to assess progress, one of which was the education level of staff. From 2007 through 2011, data we reviewed showed an improvement in the qualifications of RMI teaching staff. However, data for a key measure of student achievement, the indicator on student "proficiency" levels, were found to be unreliable, and so we were unable to make an assessment of student performance. Regarding progress in infrastructure, we noted that the RMI tracks its progress in the infrastructure sector by the completion of projects and that 200 classrooms had been constructed or renovated during the period of our review. This accomplishment, however, is not one of the RMI's 20 indicators of educational progress.

5. In its comments, the RMI suggested that we provide a more comprehensive statement on the uses of supplemental education grants and quoted an extensive definition of uses found in the fiscal procedures agreement. We edited the relevant text on page 9 in our report to address this concern.

6. In its comments regarding our site visits to various schools where we observed safety doors off their hinges or propped open because they were not properly installed, the RMI stated that the problem at Rairok Elementary School has been corrected, and that maintenance crews had started repairs at Delap, Laura, and Rita Elementary Schools. We noted this information on page 32. We have not verified this information.

7. In its comments regarding our observations regarding water tanks that were not connected to school buildings at sites we visited, the RMI stated that Ministry of Education maintenance crews were currently fixing the catchment tanks and that the tanks were intentionally disconnected for repair purposes. We noted this information on page 33. We have not verified this information.

8. In its comments regarding our visit to Laura Elementary School and its lack of power in one old building still being used, the RMI indicated that all classrooms at Laura Elementary School are hooked up to power and that Ministry of Education maintenance does not recall any complaints about the of lack of power but that some internal electrical

problem might have occurred during our visit. We noted this
information on page 33. We have not verified this information.

9. In its comments, the RMI noted that Delap Elementary School
currently has no problem with water. It noted though that during the
dryer months water catchment tanks are low or have no water, and
that Majuro Water and Sewer Company rations water. The reference
to the lack of water at Delap Elementary school was deleted from the
final report.

10. In its comments regarding our observation that a school building was
being used on Ebeye though it was considered unsafe, the RMI noted
that the building has been abandoned and that a new three-classroom
building has been constructed at Kwajalein Atoll High School. We
noted this information on page 33. We have not verified this
information.

11. In its comments, the RMI noted that the Office of the Chief Secretary
did not have the authority to withhold funds, but if it had the authority
to do so, it would do so as a last resort. We amended the text on page
51 of the report to reflect this information.

12. In its comments, the RMI stated that it feels a reference to intent of
the RMI trust fund to provide an annual source of revenue post-2023
should cite our 2007 trust fund report. We added the footnote citing
our prior trust fund report, as suggested.

Appendix XII: GAO Contact and Staff Acknowledgments

GAO Contact	David Gootnick, (202) 512-3149 or gootnickd@gao.gov
Staff Acknowledgments	In addition to the person named above, Emil Friberg (Assistant Director), Christina Bruff, Julie Hirshen, and Jeffrey Isaacs were key contributors to this report. Ashley Alley, David Dayton, Martin De Alteriis, and Etana Finkler provided technical assistance.

Related GAO Products

Compacts of Free Association: Improvements Needed to Assess and Address Growing Migration. GAO-12-64. Washington, D.C.: November 14, 2011.

Compacts of Free Association: Micronesia Faces Challenges to Achieving Compact Goals. GAO-08-859T, Washington, D.C.: June 10, 2008.

Compacts of Free Association: Implementation Activities Have Progressed, but the Marshall Islands Faces Challenges to Achieving Long-Term Compact Goals. GAO-07-1258T. Washington, D.C.: September 25, 2007.

Compacts of Free Association: Trust Funds for Micronesia and the Marshall Islands May Not Provide Sustainable Income. GAO-07-513. Washington, D.C.: June 15, 2007.

Compacts of Free Association: Micronesia's and the Marshall Islands' Use of Sector Grants. GAO-07-514R. Washington, D.C.: May 25, 2007.

Compacts of Free Association: Micronesia and the Marshall Islands Face Challenges in Planning for Sustainability, Measuring Progress, and Ensuring Accountability. GAO-07-163. Washington, D.C.: December 15, 2006.

Compacts of Free Association: Development Prospects Remain Limited for Micronesia and the Marshall Islands. GAO-06-590. Washington, D.C.: June 27, 2006.

Compacts of Free Association: Implementation of New Funding and Accountability Requirements Is Well Underway, but Planning Challenges Remain. GAO-05-633. Washington, D.C.: July 11, 2005.

Compact of Free Association: Single Audits Demonstrate Accountability Problems over Compact Funds. GAO-04-7. Washington, D.C.: October 7, 2003.

Compact of Free Association: An Assessment of Amended Compacts and Related Agreements. GAO-03-890T. Washington, D.C.: June 18, 2003.

Compact of Free Association: An Assessment of Current U.S. Proposals to Extend Assistance. GAO-02-857T. Washington, D.C.: July 17, 2002.

Foreign Assistance: Effectiveness and Accountability Problems Common in U.S. Programs to Assist Two Micronesian Nations. GAO-02-70. Washington, D.C.: January 22, 2002.

Foreign Relations: Kwajalein Atoll Is the Key U.S. Defense Interest in Two Micronesian Nations. GAO-02-119. Washington, D.C.: January 22, 2002.

Compact of Free Association: Negotiations Should Address Aid Effectiveness and Accountability and Migrants' Impact on U.S. Areas. GAO-02-270T. Washington, D.C.: December 6, 2001.

Foreign Relations: Migration From Micronesian Nations Has Had Significant Impact on Guam, Hawaii, and the Commonwealth of the Northern Mariana Islands. GAO-02-40. Washington, D.C.: October 5, 2001.

www.ingramcontent.com/pod-product-compliance
Lightning Source LLC
Chambersburg PA
CBHW080258290526
45790CB00005B/1852